K. enastone Grant

Wing Commander 'Dizzy' Allen earned his nickname when, in his early days in a fighter squadron, he managed to put his Spitfire into a flat spin. In his book of recollections he describes vividly and sympathetically the extraordinary way of life of fighter pilots, the constant proximity of death and the necessity to conceal grief for men who would never return; the friendships that were struck up within the close-knit unit of the squadron; and the moments of bawdy hilarity during hours off-duty.

After 26 years' service Wing Commander Allen retired from the RAF and then became a professional passenger as a Queen's Messenger, a job which enabled him to fly nearly a million miles and visit every corner of the earth.

Battle for Britain

The Recollections of
H. R. 'Dizzy' Allen, DFC

He flies through the air with the greatest of ease,
This daring young man on the flying trapeze;
His figure is handsome, all girls he can please,
And my love he purloined her away.

(Leybourne, *The Man on the Flying Trapeze*, 1860)

CORGI BOOKS
A DIVISION OF TRANSWORLD PUBLISHERS LTD

For my long-suffering daughter,
Cecilia Mary Anne

BATTLE FOR BRITAIN

A CORGI BOOK 0 552 09799 3

Originally published in Great Britain
by Arthur Barker Ltd.

PRINTING HISTORY
Arthur Barker edition published 1973
Corgi edition published 1975

This low-priced Corgi Book has been completely
reset in a type face designed for easy reading,
and was printed from new plates. It contains
the complete text of the original hard-cover
edition.

Corgi Books are published by
Transworld Publishers Ltd.,
Cavendish House, 57–59 Uxbridge Road,
Ealing, London W.5.
Made and printed in Great Britain by
Cox & Wyman Ltd., London, Reading and Fakenham

ACKNOWLEDGEMENTS

I am indebted to my pilot's flying logbook, an immaculate historical source if ever there was one, coupled with my fading memory. Also to my guardian angel, without whose succour I would not be here today.

CONTENTS

LIST OF ILLUSTRATIONS
Between pages 104 and 105

PREFACE

I JOINED my first squadron in May 1940. According to my pilot's logbook I then had flown 63 dual and 145 solo hours. The only aircraft types I had experience of were the Tiger Moth – my *ab initio* trainer – the Miles Magister and the North American Harvard. In other words, I was as green as an unripe strawberry. Even so, I was lucky; I still had a month or two in hand which would allow me a little time to increase my experience before the onset of Armageddon. Others were not so fortunate.

I was lucky again because my first squadron was equipped with Spitfires, one of the loveliest aircraft ever designed, possibly the superlative fighter. Its designer was R. J. Mitchell of Supermarine, and he gained his inspiration from watching seagulls in flight. They flew very gracefully, but he did not make the attempt to copy the gulls' wings; he was probably inspired in his wing design by the pigeon, one of the hardiest birds of them all and very fast in flight. Eagles would have been poor models, although they can hover for hours and swoop at devastating speed. He would never have been able to copy the vulture because, even to this day, no one quite knows how they control their extraordinary method of flight.

The Spitfire was in a different class from the Hurricane; it was a race-horse where the Hurricane was a hack. The Spitfire even had the edge over the Messerschmitt 109, or bf 109, although where Willy Messerschmitt gained his inspiration I don't know. The Spitfire compelled me to apply for a commission in the RAF. I saw it in flight, I saw photographs of it and I fell in love with it. It turned me on. There is nothing perfect in this world, I suppose, but the Spitfire came close to perfection. Women of the utmost beauty can still be faulted, so could the Spitfire. In certain of her mannerisms she was nearly as awful a bitch as the loveliest woman I ever met, who was on a par with Browning's mistress, smooth marbly limbs and all – but they were nothing like as cold as marble. The cockpit of the Spitfire was too narrow, the undercarriage was not widely spaced enough, the controls in the early models were too sensitive fore and aft, her battery of eight Browning machine-guns was inadequate against the cannon of the Me 109. She was prone to turn on to her nose if the brakes were used with too much violence. If one landed her over a filled-in bomb crater, ten to one the wheels would sink in and she would topple on to her nose – if not on to her back which was a potentially neck-breaking business.

To taxi her literally gave one a pain in the neck. She sat back on her tailwheel, and the cowlings which contained the mightily successful Merlin engine obscured one's forward vision. The only recourse was to swing her from side to side on the brakes which allowed one to see obliquely ahead. Even so, there were a number of taxiing accidents in my squadron because of the difficulties of attempting to scramble in the shortest time possible, which in theory had to be compatible with aircraft safety while on the ground. One of our pilots, on one occasion, drove his car out to his Spitfire after he heard the scramble order, and parked it a discreet distance away. He then proceeded to cut his car in half with the steel, three-bladed propeller of his Spitfire as he failed to discern the fact that while he was taxiing, his car was under the nose of his aircraft. We laughed our heads off, but it didn't do his Spitfire much good; and we were short of serviceable Spitfires.

'Air' derives from the latin *aer*. I thought I would fall in love at first sight with the Goddess *Aer* and I was mistaken. On my first flight my instructor put the Tiger Moth into a bunt and I was sick. He shouldn't have done that, but perhaps he thought I was over-confident and needed cutting down to size. He was mistaken; I was under-confident so I probably acted the part of extrovert to conceal this.

'Good God,' he said, when after landing and switching off the magnetos, he peered into my cockpit and noticed that I was covered with vomit, 'I hope you're not going to be one of those air-sick fellows.'

'Wouldn't you be,' I spluttered, 'on your first time up?'

'Better give the rigger half a crown for cleaning up the mess,' he said as he strode off to the bar.

He sent me off on my first solo flight after five hours' dual. This meant I was a fast learner as some chaps needed eight or even ten hours before going solo. But there are sage enough people who consider that the slow learner finishes the better for his longer apprenticeship, and there is truth in this. When I joined my first fighter squadron, my assessment as to pilot proficiency was above the average. One of my squadron commanders, in the course of time, assessed me as an exceptional fighter pilot. I think he was being over-kind. I never was either an exceptional or brilliant fighter pilot, although at the end of it all I was certainly as experienced as most.

But, when I landed after my first solo flight, the Tiger Moth hit the ground so hard that she bounced ten feet into the air. It was at that precise moment that I realized the Goddess *Aer* and I could only live together in a love/hate relationship. We were going to remain in such a state of unholy matrimony for nearly thirty years.

ONE

THE FIRST SQUADRON

It was only by the skin of my teeth that I managed to get what I wanted, which was to be posted to a fighter squadron after having been awarded the flying brevet. It could so easily have occurred that I was sent to fly bombers or even flying-boats. On arrival at the squadron I then knew the protocol: one salutes one's Flight Commander first thing in the morning, for example, and addresses him as 'sir'. Then one calls him George – if that happens to be his name. Last thing in the evening, the rigmarole is repeated even though one might have called him a four letter word in the interim. It is a good system and one to which I never objected. The Squadron Commander, on the other hand, was something rather different. In the first place he might easily be ten years older than oneself, and in my case he was. Then he is the local Almighty, one of the men who can make or break a junior officer.

After I had ensured that the buttons on my uniform were clean enough, I formed up for my formal and first interview with the man who commanded the squadron I had had the honour to be posted to. The Squadron Adjutant looked me over, and ushered me into the Squadron Commander's office. I could hardly see for tobacco smoke, but marched up to the desk, saluted and peered through the mist.

I dimly perceived a large and bulky man lying back in his

15

chair with his feet planted firmly on the desk. He was about thirty years of age, had started the process of balding and had blue, slightly protruding eyes. He crashed his feet to the ground, arose from his chair, shook me by the hand and then collapsed back into his previous posture. Despite his casual approach it seemed clear to me that he was a very shrewd man.

'Nice to meet you,' he said. 'Have you ever flown a Spitfire?'

'No, sir. The only monoplane I've flown was a Harvard.'

'You know all about these monoplanes then, I hope? You know all about incipient spins and that sort of thing?'

'Not in too much detail,' I replied, 'but I expect I'll learn.'

'You'd better bloody well learn mighty quick sharp and without breaking one of my Spitfires,' he said.

We chatted about this and that and he told me I was appointed to 'A' Flight; that my Flight Commander would be Flight Lieutenant Billy Bragg; that he hoped I would enjoy being with his squadron; and he hinted that I should read up something about the history of the squadron. He wished me good luck, and I saluted and left, little knowing that he was to become in the course of time one of the best friends I have ever had – or ever will have.

My next port of call was to the equipment store to be given flying equipment, such as a flying helmet, an Irving flying suit which zipped up, flying boots with wool linings thick leather gauntlets and so on. I had already checked in at the Officers' Mess, been allocated a room and signed the membership book. Then I had to rescue my car which had sighed to a halt on my arrival a mere 400 yards from the Officers' Mess. An enterprising Sergeant fitter had already hauled it into the car-park of the Sergeants' Mess and diagnosed that one of the pistons had seized up. I sold it to him for £40 which was a good enough bargain on both sides.

At 8 a.m. on the dot the next day I reported to Billy Bragg. His office was contained in a tent, he had an adequate enough desk, a locker for his flying clothing and little else. I saluted smartly and called him 'sir'. His return of my obeisance was to nod his head in acknowledgement. He was small, tough, with excellent manners, erect, a product of the RAF College at Cranwell but rather dull – he smoked a pipe. We chatted about this and that while he was reading my pilot's logbook to see what experience of the air I had gained, and he then came to his decision.

'*Flight Sergeant!*' he bawled.

A head poked round the flap of the tent, a Flight Sergeant materialized, marched to the desk, saluted, remained strictly at attention and replied:

'*Sir!*'

'At ease, Flight. This is our newly joined pilot.'

Flight Sergeant Dennis relaxed, turned to me and I shook him by the hand. He gave me a salute in return even though I was only an acting Pilot Officer.

'Flight,' Bragg said, 'could you drag out our oldest Spitfire for this new officer to make his first solo flight? What about LZ–X? Isn't that the one in need of a major overhaul in a few more flying hours?'

'That's right, sir,' Dennis replied. 'She's almost in need of a 250 hour inspection.'

'How fortuitous,' Bragg said. 'Even if he does prang it it won't matter too much. Get it ready if you would.'

Dennis saluted, gave me a grin and left.

'Anything you want to know about flying the Spitfire?' Bragg inquired.

'Not really,' I replied. 'In this business I reckon one has to find out for oneself.'

17

I went to the locker room, climbed into my flying kit, shoved the parachute on to my shoulder and staggered out to LZ-X. Billy Bragg was there waiting for me. I strapped the parachute on, scrambled on to the wing and the rigger helped me into the cockpit. Billy climbed on to the wing and gave me the cockpit drill; there were, of course, no dual control Spitfires in those days, so one's first solo flight in these aircraft was similar to one's first ever solo in a Tiger Moth. Before he jumped off the wing, Billy gave me his final words of advice.

'Keep it clearly in mind that she is extremely sensitive fore and aft.'

The Rolls-Royce Merlin engine developed over a thousand hp, and I eased the throttle open gingerly on the grass airfield. As I tentatively gave her full boost, I felt the great tug of the torque and had to wrestle with the aircraft to regain control. This aircraft was a Mark I model with a three bladed propeller, whereas the prototype had only two blades. The torque on the prototype must have been almost beyond the average man's strength to control. At this stage, one could only put the airscrew into fine pitch for take-off and landing, and coarse pitch for normal cruising. One was in bottom gear so to speak for take-off, and top gear for normal flight. Later, after suitable modifications, it was possible to control the pitch of the propeller through the whole spectrum.

LZ-X lurched over the rough field gaining speed and I eased the stick forward only to be horrified by the immediate reaction which almost caused the propeller to dig into the grass. I over-corrected and she almost fell back on to her tail wheel. Billy was quite right; she was extremely sensitive fore and aft. However, we bumped into the air and I put her into a climb. Then I had to retract the undercarriage. This was achieved on the early models by pumping with a large black lever which required about thirty vigorous pulls and pushes to do the job. I pushed and pulled on the lever until I saw the green warning lights vanish and red rights appear, meaning the undercart was fully up. Meanwhile due to my exertions the Spitfire had nosed up and down in a dangerous manner as she commenced to climb, because my muscular efforts with the right arm had affected my left hand which held the control column. I climbed, making sure my oxygen system was functioning properly, until I was at thirty thousand feet. LZ–X might well have been ready for a major maintenance inspection but to me she was my personal swallow. I rolled, I dived, I came up on the zoom and stall-turned her. She was as light as a feather on the controls, almost dangerously so. I put her into a dive and watched with satisfaction the air speed indicator build up to something over four hundred mph, much the fastest speed I had then ever achieved.

I have no words worthy of describing the Spitfire; it was an aircraft quite out of this world. There was certainly no love/hate relationship between me and my Spitfires; there was only love on my account, and on not one occasion did any of these aircraft let me down. I suffered quite grievous injuries when flying Spitfires, but they were due to my own errors or other factors, certainly not because of any fault in the design of the aircraft. I bounced on landing, but not all that badly. Certainly not badly enough to have to report a heavy landing so that checks should be made by the ground crew.

I had another familiarization flight that day and then the laborious process of training to become an operationally effective fighter pilot commenced. First I trailed behind an experienced pilot and he pointed out to me over the R/T important landmarks to assist me in my future navigation. We flew virtually by *Bradshaw* in those days, taking note of railway lines and important features such as rivers and canals. If one had the ability to fly low enough to read the name of a railway station, that was of considerable assistance. (Radio homing aids were virtually non-existent.) Then came formation flying experience, and whereas I was capable of flying in tight formation in the training aircraft I had been used to, the Spitfire was a brute with her sensitive controls. In any walk of life I have seldom had the experience of absolute despair, of coming to the conclusion that what I was attempting to do was quite beyond my capability. But in the case of learning to fly tight formation with the Spitfire Mark I, I remember vividly a feeling of utter hopelessness, that such missions were impossible of achievement, that I would never learn the art. My formation leader's aircraft was flying straight and level, but to me it was jumping up and down like a frog; then it would skid towards my Spitfire and I would have to take drastic remedial action. I was, of course, over-correcting. The art of formation flying relies not only on an ability to handle the aircraft with the minimum use of controls and engine throttle, but is almost entirely anticipatory.

However, after an initial sensation of despair and dismay, with a little more experience the process then became so natural that I could hardly believe I suffered such original despondency. I could, in the course of time, almost make my wing-tip touch the fuselage of his aircraft behind my formation leader's wing. I knew very well that I was capable of rubbing my wingtip against his in the air with such delicacy that the paintwork would have showed the marks. Indeed, I very nearly had to on one occasion, which was when Billy Bragg took off with me and another pilot and ran himself into the worst cumulo-nimbus (thundercloud) in almost the whole of my experience. This occurred, in fact, due to poor airmanship on his part.

As the grey of the cloud turned to jet black, as the rain hissed down with drops the size of tennis balls, the only thing to do was to get closer and closer to Billy's Spitfire until my wingtip was almost rubbing against his perspex cockpit canopy despite the extreme turbulence. Even then I began to lose sight of his aircraft and appreciated that we were now in an impossible and extremely dangerous situation. I remained in formation as long as possible, as my own ability to fly on instruments in conditions of such turbulence was non-existent. But when the moment of truth arrived, I banked to starboard with such force as to make my artificial horizon, which was gyroscopically controlled, topple, and I then had no orientation at all. For whatever reason I hauled back on the stick and because of the attitude of my Spitfire this caused me to nose dive towards the ground as if one were performing the final manoeuvre of a loop. I could of course see nothing except the black of the cloud, but I maintained the pressure on the stick because I could think of nothing else to do. The altimeter was turning down so fast as to make no sense; the other flight instruments were no longer of any value.

I came out of that cloud with an airspeed of over 450 mph and saw the green of the ground dimly through a thunderous cloudburst. I could have been at no more than six hundred feet above ground level when I broke cloud. Another few seconds would have been enough to plough me and my Spitfire thirty feet under the soil. I broke into a heavy sweat as I reduced speed, found out where I was, and ambled back to base – thoughtfully.

Billy landed ten minutes after I did. We did not discuss the incident. But I learned about flying from that.

Flying terrified me, but there was a curious juxtaposition of emotions because I loved the whole business of taking to the air with the hope of landing again. But I hated, loathed and detested night flying and this was probably due to the fact that I was not only slightly short-sighted but lacked adequate night vision. I am no oculist although I know quite a lot about aero-medical problems. What I also know is that adequate night vision does not necessarily have anything to do with short- or long-sightedness, it is a problem on its own. In the war they used to say that eating carrots improved one's night vision, but the *raison d'être* there was probably based on the farming industry, the amount of carrots produced, and hence the need for the general public to eat them in quantity. In any case, the Spitfire was a most objectionable aircraft to have to fly at night. It had for a start a long nose – it had to have a long nose to contain the horsepower of the incredibly successful Merlin engine. But it had short stub exhaust pipes which were perfect by day but killers by night. By day one could scan easily beyond the exhaust stubs; by night, one would see only the whole apparatus of the effluent left by the Merlin. At dusk as one took to the air, the previously invisible exhausted gases would begin to show in the form of blue flames. As night encroached, those blue flames would turn into fiery red flames and furthermore the exhaust-pipes would gleam bright red, showing the temperature at which they had to work. All this was blinding on the final approach and landing, and when combined with the long nose of the Spitfire, made the situation almost impossible.

But whether this is a fair summary of the problem or not, Billy Bragg quite rightly decided in due course that the time was ripe for me to take off and land in a Spitfire at night. The landing aids were primitive enough which exacerbated the difficulties, and consisted of a Chance light which flashed in morse code an indication of the position of our particular airfield. The only other aid was the officer in charge of night flying who had as his vital instruments an Aldis lamp which could show either a green light, meaning you were OK, or a red light meaning you were in difficulty; he also had in his hand a Verey pistol which could shoot off green, red or white cartridges which exploded when at their zenith, all of which contained a life or death message. The flare path for a night take-off in those days consisted of paraffin-soaked wads of cotton wool or some such material, placed in tin canisters, situated on either side of the take-off run on the grass airfield. Some unfortunate chap had to walk a distance of more than a thousand yards and back again to light them up.

According to orders I taxied my Spitfire out to the start of the flare-path one dark night, having first dimmed down the cockpit lights which would otherwise have blinded me. The paraffin flares indicated the line of take-off, calculated previously according to the direction of the wind. I lined up LZ–X, gingerly opened the throttle and in due course gave her full boost. I gently hauled her off the ground when my instinct gave me the message that this was the appropriate moment – I would not allow my eyes to flicker in the direction of the airspeed indicator and be deflected from the flare path – and climbed into the night air. Whereupon I was immediately lost. Our nearest large town was Cambridge but, of course, it was blacked out as there was a war on – so I could take no heed of Cambridge. I remembered the course I set according to the compass for take-off, turned on a reciprocal heading and, with great good luck, saw below me the paraffin lights indicating that I was over my airfield. I climbed to about fifteen thousand feet, most certainly did not indulge in any manoeuvre which would cause my artificial horizon to topple, and burned off some of the hundred octane fuel in the tanks of the Spitfire to ease the problem of landing.

Then I slowly lost height, joined the airfield circuit – there was no radio communication between me and the ground – appreciated in what direction I should attempt to land because they had an arrow lit with paraffin to give one that indication; flew downwind in the circuit and began my final descent prior to landing LZ–X. I kept the flare path in view until I suddenly realized that I could no longer see it ahead. Simultaneously, a red Verey cartridge exploded in the air; I opened the throttle and climbed a little higher – whereupon I saw the flare path once again. I crossed the threshold and plonked her down on her main undercarriage leaving the tailwheel to drop when she felt like it.

Ken was the officer in charge of night flying. As I climbed out of the cockpit covered with sweat, he approached me.

'Feeling all right?' he inquired.

'Good enough.'

'Do you know,' he said, 'that you were within five feet of the ground when I shot off that Verey cartridge. Do you know that if there had been an ordinary old elm tree in your path, it would have been curtains for you?'

As with most things in life, the men in the squadron were more important than the machines. A fighter squadron in those days consisted of about twenty aircraft, with a couple in war reserve, and probably two hundred airmen together with twenty or so pilots. The more senior pilots tended to have their personal aircraft reserved for them, save when their Spitfires had to go into the hangars for inspections, but as I was just part of the sediment at that time I had to take any Spitfire that happened to be available. The Spitfire, through unfortunate decisions taken about 1934, was a comparatively rare aircraft in early 1940; indeed there was only one of the breed in squadron service at the time of the Munich 'agreement'. And although my squadron was one of the first to be re-equipped from Gauntlets with Spitfires, none of the pilots had much flying experience on the type although some of them were very experienced pilots by the standards of the day.

These men whom I got to know so intimately more than thirty years ago are, in the main, shadowy figures in my memory today. Most of them are dead – killed in action, and I met only a few of the remainder later in the war and afterwards. There was a tall buffoon, of Scottish ancestry, by name MacLeod, who had a certain charm but on the whole was exceedingly dim. The latter defect probably came about because he had been a considerable pugilist when at school and had possibly suffered brain damage all unbeknown either to him or the school doctors. His nose was broken – not unnaturally – and he had a few false teeth to replace those that had been knocked out in the boxing ring. He kept thinking he was flying a Gauntlet when he was by now flying Spitfires. In consequence, he had lapses and kept forgetting to lower his undercarriage on landing – the Gauntlet had a non-retractable undercart. After three belly-landings he was summoned to appear before the Air Officer Commanding, given a formal rebuke, and was asked to pay £5 for the damage caused by his negligence. This was quite a lot of money then, but as he had achieved something like £1,000 worth of damage to the three Spitfires, it was a light enough sentence. I never remember quite what happened to MacLeod; he seemed simply to vanish in the night.

Then there was Tom Brickall who bred bull-terriers – dogs, incidentally, which had an enormous appeal to fighter pilots for some obscure reason – obscure, save perhaps that they are about the toughest animals on four legs for their weight. Tom at the time clearly could not have the use of a kennel for his breeding activities, but he solved the problem very adequately by purchasing a little Austin Seven which he used as his mobile kennel. He also preferred to have his wife with him, and as all the official married quarters were then being used for offices and the like, I believe he kept her in another car as another form of mobile kennel.

Bill Marlin became one of my closest friends on the squadron and he went on to have a brilliant war finishing up with a DFC and two bars. Bill had originated from Lancashire and one could still detect a trace of the local dialect if one listened with a keen enough ear. He was a couple of years older than myself, had considerably greater flying experience, and possessed of a roman nose and slightly protruding teeth. He had a red face and curling hair, was tallish, burly and tough. The thing I remember most about him was that he almost always appeared to be smiling. He was a natural marksman: I should know; I was flying with him one day when he blew the canopy off a Me 109 at about four hundred yards, which was the extreme range with our batteries of .303 Brownings. The German pilot soared out of his cockpit – they had a primitive form of ejector seat – did a couple of somersaults in the air and then I saw his parachute open. We didn't bother to follow him down to see where he finished up, and in any case we then had to ward off the punitive attacks being made on us by his colleagues.

Ken Boyle was another pilot I remember vividly. He was short, dapper, always had his hair slicked well down with some sort of brilliantine, was the best shot against the drogue in the whole of Fighter Command, had rabbity teeth and very considerable charm. He was, in fact, an exceptional pilot, but, alas, he was killed in action, as I shall describe in due course. Ken was a rare asset to a squadron socially because he could play the piano with great expertise; I believe he was self-taught. Anything that entered one's mind Ken could play on request, whether a pornographic RAF ballad or Chopin. His ability to play *Stardust* – one of the hit tunes of the day – was beyond description. Then he would turn to a classical nocturne without a change of expression either on his face or via his fingers on the keyboard. I was utterly horrified one day when Ken never returned; it was one of the greatest tragedies in my experience.

But looming large in my memory is the figure of my Squadron Commander, Jasper Gillies, more of whom later. I once calculated the mean age of the pilots we had in the squadron in 1940 – it worked out to be twenty-one years, despite the fact that Jasper was approaching the age of thirty. In the RAF before the war, officers in the General Duties Branch had to specialize in some subject or other as they advanced up the promotional ladder. One could become an engineer, an armament specialist, for example, or a flying instructor. Jasper plunged for flying instruction and this might have affected his operational effectiveness as a fighter pilot. What I mean is that he was an extremely effective Squadron Commander, a fighter leader *par excellence* with claims to several German kills. He could, however, possibly have done better in the latter sense had he not previously been a flying instructor, which work demands precise and accurate flying on all occasions and a concentration on the requirements of one's pupil to the exclusion of a coarseness of aircraft handling which is necessary in combat conditions.

If, for example, one is flying with the slip and turn indicator perfectly balanced – which is essential in flying instruction – one might be easy meat to an attacking German fighter. On the other hand, if one's aircraft is yawing under pressures brought about by rough use of the rudder bars, this would increase the difficulties for the German who was taking him. Additionally, flying instruction is a deliberate, calculated process, whereas fighter combat is making the best possible use of heavy boots on the rudder bars or, in short, opportunism combined with quick reflexes. To put it another way, if one has achieved a successful tour as a flying instructor, one ought to take in a flying course oneself to unlearn the arts of instructing before joining a fighter squadron. There is theory and there are the practical applications and the two are not necessarily compatible.

I had been on the squadron less than a month when I was given the nickname which has been with me ever since. Nicknames come easily in fighter squadrons, as for example

'Chalky' White or 'Dusty' Miller. Not so easily explained was one given to a chum of mine, 'Dirty' Williams, except by saying that he was a devil with the women. One day, I managed to put my Spitfire into a flat spin and only God knows how I did it. It is a most difficult attitude from which to recover and I was lucky to recover from it. The news got around, which combined with a fairly wild approach to life brought the nickname 'Dizzy'.

TWO

OPERATIONAL APPRENTICE

My squadron operated over Dunkirk, took note of blazing Rotterdam, lost a few pilots and used the forward base at Martlesham Heath for its fighter sweeps. According to my pilot's logbook I later engaged in combat for the first time on 19th June, 1940. Although I did not appreciate it then, this was probably the most hazardous engagement I ever had with a German aircraft. Radar, or Radio Direction Finding (RDF), as it was then called, was generally fairly inadequate, but on this occasion it worked perfectly. Three of us were scrambled on an interception course and found a Junkers 88 no less than sixty miles out to sea. This was a very fast German bomber and it led us a dance for another ten or so miles before we could engage, and only then in the form of a dead astern attack which is of itself fairly dangerous, as the Ju 88 was provided with effective defensive armament. Billy Bragg opened fire first, well out of range, and vanished from my field of vision. I opened fire at probably eight hundred yards in the belief that I was within firing range, but thereby having not the slightest prospect of hitting the bomber. The number three in the section did his best but we were all hopelessly undertrained in fighter combat and the Ju 88 sped home to its Dutch airfield. Indeed, the German pilot then reported – according to British Air intelligence – that his gunner had shot down two Spitfires on this occasion!

The reason why this was a hazardous operation from our point of view was that there would have been very little prospect of ever seeing England, Home and Beauty once again had a chance bullet from the Ju 88's guns even so much as caused the coolant tanks in our Spitfires to leak. This thought hardly occurred to me at the time; it slowly evolved in my mind with further experience how very vulnerable an engine reliant on glycol cooling was; an air cooled radial engine is nothing like as vulnerable.

But our main duty at this stage was flying over convoys to protect them against sudden assaults from the Luftwaffe. The ships were usually little coalers plying between Newcastle and London, and all in all wasted a great number of flying hours which should have been utilized in a fierce training programme. Although it is true that a maritime nation like Britain depends on sea communications, the coastal convoys should have been stopped much earlier than they were.

Round and round the convoys we would fly, bored almost to tears, for up to forty-five minutes until our relief pilots arrived. To gain some respite from the sheer boredom, I would fly as low as I dared, attempting, almost but not quite, to cause my propeller blades to flick the sea. The only distraction came via the radio in my Spitfire which, at that time, worked on high frequency bands. This one would tune in on the waveband one preferred, and I preferred Henry Hall and his BBC Orchestra. I would listen to the hit tunes of the day, hour after hour, day in day out. And then what happened? They removed our HF radios and gave us VHF sets which worked on set frequencies selected by pressing one of four buttons. This meant I could no longer tune in to Henry Hall. I nearly went mad.

It was on 30th August when I was involved in my first successful combat under the leadership of an experienced

Sergeant Pilot. It might appear to have been a fairly crazy organization which allowed NCOs to take under their command officer pilots, but it worked very well at the time. The section leader was in total command in the air no matter what his rank, and to be handed the responsibility of a Section Leader depended purely and simply on one's personal flying experience. At this stage there were a considerable number of NCO pilots, approximately 35 per cent of the total pilots in Fighter Command I would estimate, many of whom had achieved a considerable number of flying hours. These men were hand picked and were normally tradesmen, many of whom had gained their mechanical skills at the RAF apprentices' school based on Halton near Wendover. This was an excellent technical college and even to gain entry demanded pretty high scholastic standards. To be creamed off after entry from a course of some two hundred apprentices and recommended for pilot duties was a very considerable achievement. To rise to this pinnacle meant that you had to be good, you had to be good, you had to be good.

Pilots, of course, regardless of nationality, have an affinity which is almost unique among the professional classes. They share the same dangers, work in the same medium of the air, get closer to God therefore, and take the same risks. On the ground it was a curious situation when, as in this particular case, a hardened Irish Flight Sergeant was given authority to have me and Pickles, both of us Pilot Officers, under his command. He could not command us on the ground as we, so to speak, commanded him. So his brief demanded a certain amount of tact. The Irish are not necessarily well known for tact but he was an artist in that field.

We were ordered to come to readiness. Waiting by my Spitfire, I saw the Section Commander step on to his wing, so I attached my parachute, my rigger, Briggs, heaved my backside as I scrambled on to the wing and I settled into the

31

cockpit. It is very boring sitting in the cockpit of an aircraft waiting for something to happen when nothing does – but that did not occur on this occasion. Almost immediately after I was settled in, having primed the petrol pump for immediate starting, checked the rudder and elevator trim controls, a red Verey light exploded high in the air fired from the Duty Pilot's hut. The mechanics immediately switched on the starter battery, I pressed the appropriate knob, and the engine fired first go. I was the number two in the section and Pickles number three; he came running out of the dispersal hut as he had decided to stay at readiness there but, on the other hand, he was a champion sprinter which I certainly was not. I waited for the Flight Sergeant's Spitfire to move forward and then followed. In my mirror I saw Pickles catching up fast behind me, smoke pouring from his exhaust tubes. We took off in vic formation, transferred to the interception frequency and I listened.

'Bandit flying at over twenty thousand feet, in the area of Smith's Knoll lightship. Climb to angels twenty-five on a heading 040 degrees,' the controller stated.

'Understood,' my Flight Sergeant replied.

We closed in tight on his Spitfire and accompanied him in the climb. I checked that my oxygen system was working properly, adjusted the gun-sight for brilliance and wondered when I should turn the gunbutton on to *Fire*. The controller kept changing our course to steer and it was obvious that the bandit was making a reconnaissance sweep from north to south. The Flight Sergeant continued to gain height and levelled off when we arrived at an altitude of twenty-five thousand feet; I saw the East Anglian coastline below and then we were over the sea. The controller kept adjusting our course and my only job was to stay in close formation on my section leader. We climbed and we dived as the controller ordered, but remained one entity. Pickles was very long-sighted and he spotted the bandit long before I could see it.

32

'Tally Ho!' he exclaimed over his R/T. 'Bandit at nine o'clock, slightly below.'

'Understood,' the Section Leader replied. There was a pause of a few seconds. 'I see it,' he said. 'Line astern formation – *Go*.'

I broke to starboard and then skidded into position behind him and slightly below. Pickles waited a moment and then broke to port and came up behind me. I throttled back to make the attack formation looser and therefore more flexible. Pickles, no doubt, did likewise although I could no longer see him. We closed on the German bomber and I recognized it as a Dornier 17 from my recollection of the aircraft identifying charts which covered the pilots' room in the dispersal hut. It was known as the 'Flying Pencil', was long with twin engines and a dorsal gun turret. It looked to me to be black and, in some inexplicable way, un-British.

The Section Leader closed range. 'Am making an initial attack from the port quarter,' he said over the R/T, his voice, despite the Irish lilt, absolutely clear.

I watched him make his attack, saw smoke issuing as he fired his guns, hoped he had killed the rear gunner and then put my port wing down and dived into the attack. The Dornier was very much larger in my gunsight than in the case of my previous encounter with a Junkers bomber, meaning I was at much closer range. I pressed the gun button and nothing happened, so I hastily looked down and found that it was still on *Safe*. I switched it on to *Fire* and pressed it again. There was a noise similar to thick jute being torn apart by a giant and I saw the tracer mixed up in the ammunition load hurtle in the general direction of the Do 17. I thought I hit the rear gunner straight in the eye, but I was apparently mistaken in this appreciation. I used all my ammunition in an attack which finished up dead astern, and as there was no return fire it occurred to me that I had finished the bomber off. I hauled my Spitfire up and watched as Pickles came in for his attack. Smoke showed from his machine-gun ports and he finished firing at about a hundred yards range.

Pickles' Spitfire disappeared from my vision and I watched the Do 17. Smoke was pouring from one engine. Then, with a horrifying gentleness, it slowly turned on its back and went into a vertical dive. I followed it down and saw it strike the sea with an awful disintegration, combined with a great plume of sea water, followed by a slick of oil and then I saw yellow objects floating. These must have been the dinghies intended for air sea rescue operation. I felt sick, but a certain exhilaration overcame that in short time.

I could see the aircraft of neither the section leader nor Pickles, so I radioed a message indicating my position and calling for air sea rescue forces, if any, to attempt to pick up any of the German crew who might be still alive and presumably swimming. The controller acknowledged saying he would do his best. Then I turned on to a heading of 270 degrees and made my way back to base. The Flight Sergeant had landed ten minutes ahead of me having lost sight of the Do 17 after his initial attack. But there was no Pickles. Indeed, I did not see Pickles for another three days until he arrived back to the squadron in a Royal Navy car.

On the attack Pickles was last man in, and I obviously had not killed the rear gunner. Pickles came in at close range and the gunner gave him a dirty great burst of fire. I expect that Pickles then killed the rear gunner; for that matter, I expect that he also shot down the Do 17 from his own burst of fire with his close range attack. This, of course, was impossible to prove as all three of us had fired long bursts at the German aircraft and anyone of us might have delivered the lethal blow; so we shared this kill. But I did not have to share the awful experience Pickles then had to endure because the German gunner's bullets hit his coolant tank, his engine seized up and he had no recourse but to glide as far as he could over the sea, losing height in the meantime. He spotted a lightship, circled it and belly-landed as near to it as possible. But the trouble with the Spitfire when belly-landing it on the sea was that its large radiator and other configurations scooped up water at the moment of impact, caused it almost immediately to nose-down in the water and head towards the sea-bed at a high rate of descent.

Pickles' moment of truth, accordingly, arrived when he was so deep in the water before he could get his safety harness unlocked, that the colour of the sea had turned from green to black. He was drowning, but he somehow or other burst free from his cockpit, gave himself a hefty shove which, fortunately, also removed his flying-boots, and soared to the surface just before the weight of the water in his lungs would have killed him. He was unconscious when the crew of the lightship dragged him out of the sea, but he came to after they administered artificial respiration. They signalled for a MTB from Harwich which took him back ashore and on into a bunk in a Naval hospital. He was in an excited state of mind when he returned to our airfield but then Pickles was always in an excited state – he was a typical fighter pilot.

The Air Ministry gave him a monetary allowance to buy a new uniform and other accoutrements to replace those which had been ruined in this near fatal incident. They refused adamantly, however, to replace his wristwatch. I remember that watch very well; it was an excellent wristwatch, with a gold case, kept good time and had been given to him as a twenty-first birthday present. Pickles had been very proud of his watch. The Air Ministry said that they could only give him an allowance of five pounds for a watch destroyed in action – as his had been – whereas his parents must have paid something over fifty pounds for their son's watch. My hatred for the bureaucratic mind, which I retain to this day, commenced without any question at that moment.

On 19th August Peter Todd had been killed, shot down by a German rear gunner in a similar manner to Pickles. Peter was my best friend on the squadron and, in a platonic fashion, I loved him dearly. He was tall and gangling with an old face, a bit of a poseur, something of a spoilt boy and comparatively rich. He had a powerful, flash touring car and whenever the squadron was moved from one airfield to another, he would attach his skis, which for some strange reason he retained, to the roof. At this stage, Norwich was our local town as we had moved from the Cambridge area, and a very nice town Norwich was before the Luftwaffe bust it wide open in a *Baedeker* raid. The girls were particularly splendid, although I did not indulge in sexual licentiousness at this time, probably in the optimistic hope that I would be all the more virile for that when the real moment came. There was a pub or club there with the name *The Adam and Eve*. I forgot whether it had a crest or not, but if it did it should have been designed with a fig-leaf, an apple, a serpent and a honeymoon.

Peter and I would, as and when we could get away from the station, take a meal in a decent hotel in Norwich. The food in such establishments early in 1940 was of a surprisingly high quality compared with the stuff they hand out today. Our favourite was *escalope de veau garnie*, and I remember Peter one evening complaining bitterly that it was insufficiently *garnie*. It was a monastic sort of life we lived in those days, curiously enough. The company was all male for a start and the hours of work equated with those put in at a monastery. We certainly didn't have to get up in the small hours to pray, but we often had to be at readiness when first light glimmered on the horizon, and this occurs half an hour

36

before dawn. For that matter, we might have had to be at readiness all through the night, depending on moon conditions, and then without respite assume operational readiness again at first light. I never heard any member of the squadron complain about the working conditions, nor did we go on strike. Monasticism, to my mind, is an ascetic condition demanding that one lives apart from the rest of the world. We fighter pilots lived apart from the world, and by this analogy, Peter was my brother living within my community.

Then they killed him; but it took three weeks before his body was washed up in the Thames estuary. Someone had to identify the body and I suggested that it would be appropriate enough if I took on the job. The body was bloated, decaying, green but it could have been no one else's body except Peter's. I signed the certificate and simultaneously tried not to vomit but with small success. On my return to the station, it was necessary for a member of the squadron to attend his burial service, so I flew the squadron Miles Magister down to an airfield near his home. His parents had arranged for a car to pick me up. I was, of course, wearing my best uniform, and my best cap flew on the rear seat of the Magister ready for me to wear when assisting in the ceremonial. The funeral service was simple, absolutely English, and I saluted the coffin as it was deposited six feet down in the earth. His mother was incredibly brave but his father crumpled slightly towards the end. Peter was, after all, his only son.

My Squadron Commander, Jasper, should never have joined the RAF. He was deeply musical although he played the piano very badly. He should have been a conductor of an orchestra; his soul was filled with music. At this time we were not performing fighter operations on any great scale and the hazards, apart from one or two engagements, were slight. Things down in Eleven Group, however, were beginning to warm up as the Luftwaffe sized up the defensive ability of Fighter Command – which wasn't too impressive in fact. Accordingly, we began to feel a sense of frustration and Jasper had to make the attempt to control us. This is where Ken and his piano came in useful, and whereas Jasper preferred to be alone in the music room while Ken strummed Chopin's delightful nocturnes and the like – 'Mr. Chop' was the wording used by Jasper when he demanded more and more Chopin – we would occasionally leave the bar and arrive in the music room, much to Jasper's chagrin. Not that we left our beer in the bar, we held it in our hands in pint tankards. Then the bawdy songs would begin.

I have in my possession *The Airman's Song Book* published in 1945, given to me by my wife with the inscription 'in the hope you may learn the cleaner versions'. It is, of course, an expurgated version of the real thing. Its range covers *Before the First World War; From 1914 to the Armistice; The 'Peace' Years 1918 to 1939;* and *The Second World War*. In their monasteries monks have their chants; in the monastic life of the flying services airmen have their songs. That there is an affinity is obvious as most of the songs of the airmen are based on the tunes to be found in *Hymn's Ancient and Modern*. The affinity ends there; our songs are sacrilegious, blasphemous, crude and inevitably contain sexual undertones.

The expurgated version of one song in the *The Airman's Song Book*, for example, contains the wording 'Bless them all, Bless them all ...' The true wording is: 'Fuck them all, fuck them all, the long and the short and the tall,' etc. These songs are often morbid as, for instance, *The Dying Airman*. Here follow a few of the verses:

Two valve springs you'll find in my stomach,
Three spark plugs are safe in my lung,

The prop is in splinters inside me,
To my fingers the joy-stick has clung.

Another one goes like this:

Take the propeller boss out of my liver,
Take the aileron out of my thigh,
From the seat of my pants take the piston,
Then see if the old crate will fly.

That the monastic life led by flying men, stuck away in airfields in remote rural areas in Britain, or in the deserts of Mesopotamia, was recognized as such is also reflected in the great number of songs to do with nuns and monks. Here is one crude enough version:

There was a monk of great renown,
He fucked the women around the town,
A dirty old bugger was he, etc.

But airmen are not inevitably pornographic in their music and lyrics; they are also, or some of them are, poets of considerable merit. This is also understandable because the air contains not only wailing spooks but is also filled with poetry. Let me give but a few examples:

So you can stay in the clouds, boy,
You can let your soul go onwards,
You have no ties on earth,
You could never have accomplished
Anything. Your ideas and ideals
Were too high. So you can stay
In the sky, boy, and have no fear.

Another:

Give them their wings:
They cannot fly too high or far
To fly above
The dirty-moted, bomb-soured, world-tired world.
And if they die they'll die,
As you should know,
More swiftly, cleanly, star-defined, than you will ever
feel.

So, life in the Squadron veered from one extreme to another, from drunkenness to sobriety, from sacrilegious ballads to Chopin, from *escalope de veau garnie* to sausages and mash in the messing tent. On one occasion, for example, I was not only officer in charge of night flying but also Orderly Officer and my problem became how to combine these duties. I gave the night flying requirement first priority and it was my wont personally to drive the enormous Chance light towed behind a three ton lorry, together with a gang of airmen, out to the selected site. For this purpose, I wore a leather fur-lined jacket and flying boots. Having completed that task, my next chore was to inspect the airmen detailed for fire picket duties. Then along came the Station Commander, who was not only one of the most stupid men I ever met in my life, but also failed to take any part in operational flying. He called me to one side.

'What the hell do you think you're doing dressed like that? The Orderly Officer must wear his best uniform for the twenty-four hours of his stint of duty. Surely you know that?'

I gazed at him like he had a hole in his brain, which of course he had.

'As a matter of fact, sir,' I replied, 'I've just been putting the Chance light on its site.'

40

'Surely another officer could have done that?'

'Possibly. But we do have officer pilots on night flying stand-by. We are, in fact, very short of officers for station duties.'

Whereupon he shut up.

But if the Station Commander was a silly old buffer, my Squadron Commander, Jasper, was anything but. He was a product of the RAF College at Cranwell, and he commanded mainly by using his charm and courtesy, but he could be stern enough if the occasion warranted. Jasper had a poker face which, indeed, gave him some financial reward as we played poker quite often on slack days. He was, however, one of the most generous men I have ever met and he would squander his hard-earned winnings by buying beer when we went to the pub. Despite his poker face, as I got to know Jasper better and better, I found he was deeply emotional. He felt the loss of his pilots more and more as time went on but his first and essential duty was however to maintain the morale of the pilots in the squadron, so he had to remain expressionless.

To his light touch we reacted accordingly. We were as wild as wild. Despite our high respect for the squadron and its traditions, we would now and again go beserk. One of the tricks, for example, was to try and topple over the small bus we used to get from the mess to the squadron dispersal hut. This was surprisingly easy to do. With perhaps a dozen men sitting in the back, it was necessary only to swing our bodies in unison and with some force and the bus would begin to lurch dangerously. They did this to me one day when I was driving, whereupon I exacerbated the lurch by turning the steering wheel in consonance thereby shifting the bus on to two wheels and then beyond. While I still had some control of the brakes, I almost stopped before we toppled over into a ditch. One chap got a cracked rib, but that apart we heaved the bus back on its wheels and proceeded on our way.

Then someone bought the book *No Orchids for Miss Blandish* by Hadley Chase, others bought further copies until there were sufficient for us all to read it quite quickly. We began to use the East Side jargon of New York just like Chase's gangsters with their over-large heads, doped and quick on the draw. It seems incredible today but everyone spoke with nasal New York accents on almost every occasion except the very formal ones. Jasper became known as 'The Boss', for example, and one enterprising chap used to wear a toy pistol in a shoulder holster. Even over the R/T, when we spotted a German aircraft, the immediate response would be – after the formalities of 'Tally Ho' on sighting had been completed – 'We get this bum, boss! We get him good!' Jasper would then tell us to shut up; he was strict about the misuse of the R/T.

By this time the Battle of Britain was warming up in the Eleven Group area, but not for us as we were deployed in the Twelve Group sector which covered East Anglia and beyond. France had fallen by now and Air Intelligence was sending us charts showing the assumed range of the bombers of the Luftwaffe and their escorting fighters. According to these diagrams the Luftwaffe could strike, for example, at Liverpool in daylight and with adequate fighter escort. This, in fact, was nonsense and produced an air of panic within the hierarchy. The assumptions rested on the belief that the twin engine, long range Messerschmitt 110 was an adequate escort fighter even against the single-engined Hurricanes and Spitfires of Fighter Command. Such conclusions merely indicated the paucity of intellect of those in high command. And, almost without question, these false premises underlay the poor deployment of the squadrons in Fighter Command when the Luftwaffe made its onslaught which, for instance, kept us in East Anglia for too long.

THREE

ELEVEN GROUP

WE kicked our heels in Twelve Group, then a signal arrived at the end of August ordering us to re-deploy to Kenley, near Croydon. Jasper had to work out a movement order; it was a complicated business moving station permanently in those days. Each move seriously reduced our operational effectiveness until such time as all our resources had been re-assembled. Yet, my squadron was moved to nine RAF stations on a 'permanent' basis within a period of no more than nine months. In most of these moves, it was impossible to discern any logic, let alone military logic. Perhaps worse than this, it means we had continuously to discover new pubs with the kind of atmosphere we preferred.

Although we were going to perform merely a ferry flight to Kenley our guns were, of course, fully armed. En route we overflew the airfield at North Weald blazing from a recent bombing raid, joined circuit and landed at Kenley. The place was a shambles; there were burned-out petrol bowsers littering the periphery of the airfield, hulks of destroyed Hurricanes and craters everywhere. We taxied to our allotted squadron dispersal and disembarked from our Spitfires. A highly agitated Squadron Leader, commander of the squadron we were relieving, greeted Jasper; he was suffering from nervous exhaustion and there was also a tic working furiously on his face. He began to give Jasper some sort of briefing when the air-raid sirens mooed their message.

'You can have the bastards,' he exclaimed. 'We're off!'

He sprinted to his aircraft followed by his squadron pilots. White smoke issued from the exhaust stubs and the squadron was in the air quicker than whores' drawers come down on Boat Race night. I make no further comment save to reiterate that nervous exhaustion had clearly set in.

We walked to the squadron dispersal hut and behind it was the fuselage of a crashed Dornier 17. I inspected it and for the first time recognized the peculiar stench that German aircraft always seemed to possess; however, the stink of death might have been mixed up with the smell of the aircraft. We drove to the mess to sort ourselves out and stood to one side as a coffin was carried out. In my room there was a shaving brush still covered with lather together with a razor. The wardrobe contained another man's clothes and I requested that they be removed. Then we sorted out the arrangements whereby we could become part of the front line of Eleven Group.

In due course we were placed at two minutes' readiness and we did not have long to wait; a red Verey cartridge soared high into the sky, and off we went in a vain attempt to give protection to British air space. We were as raw as green potatoes and the Messerschmitt 109 pilots were still flying their deadly *Jagdgeschwader* tactics so competently learned over the Iberian peninsula during the Spanish Civil War.

Our inadequacy can be illustrated statistically. I don't remember whether any of our squadron pilots claimed German kills on our first sortie from an airfield in Eleven Group: if so it does not appear in the reference books. But our first major operational sortie could hardly be described as a success because this is what happened:

Pilot A: shot down in flames by bf 109; pilot baled out with severe wounds and burns.

Pilot B: shot down by bf 109, forced landing; pilot slightly wounded.

Pilot C: ditto.

Pilot D: ditto.

Pilot E: shot down by bf 109; pilot baled out with severe wounds, and died on 6th September, 1940.

Allowing for others of our Spitfires which were hit but the pilots of which escaped injury, we lost approximately sixty per cent of the squadron in under half an hour. The fact of the matter was that we were being engaged in combat after the Luftwaffe had gained local air superiority over the Eleven Group area, which they achieved on about 1st September, 1940.

I always tried to lay my hands on LZ–X, and in the course of time I was given, so to speak, the title to this particular aircraft. It was an act of superstition, of course, and whereas airmen are nothing like as superstitious as sailors, there is no harm in life insurance. So LZ–X was important to me – not the particular aircraft because I wrecked so many of them – but the letters painted on the fuselage. I also carried a charm – a Cornish pixie made of brass – and I freely confess I used to pray, although I was never a religious man. One had to have, or so I believed, assistance from divine providence to survive. In short, God became a good friend of mine in the course of time, and I began to trust Him, although He let me down now and again. But I suppose that even God is not infallible.

The first time He let me down was on 5th September, 1940, according to my pilot's log book, when we were engaged with the *Jagdgeschwader* and I was closing on a Me 109. I had no particular hatred for the Germans but I just wanted to blow the head off this particular pilot because he was flying over British air space and he had no right to be there. I suppose I was too excited to maintain my wariness and forgot to look in my mirror. So at the same time as I was easing myself into firing range, a few of his colleagues were doing likewise to me. They were, in fact, up-sun of me and the sun is a fighter pilots most deadly enemy. They struck before I had the chance to press my firing button. The first thing I knew was that there was a stink of cordite in the cockpit, that I had a pain in one of my legs, and that I had better get the hell out, which I did.

Having half-rolled and dived vertically, I saw Kenley loom up on the horizon, and I joined circuit. Then I found that only one of my ailerons was working which made the situation fairly hazardous. But I was very soothing to LZ–X on the final approach and we both got down in one piece, although I thought at one moment that she was going to spin in. When they examined LZ–X they immediately classified her category three, meaning she was a write-off, and she had to be removed on an articulated vehicle to the factory so that whatever bits still worked could be salvaged and the residue scrapped. It was a pity, so it was. She never let me down; I let her down. But I was terrified out of my wits when they showed me the main cable which controlled the elevators. In its normal condition it was comprised of a dozen strands of high tensile steel wire all twirled around each other – no gorilla could possibly have torn it apart. But my elevator was hanging on by a single thread, and I had not only dived her at about five hundred mph, I had also hauled her out with considerable G forces when I was about six hundred feet from the ground. *Santa Maria!*

Then one of the happiest periods in my memory commenced, although at that time I would never have projected my thoughts in any such manner. We were ordered, for some quite inexplicable reason, to make a 'permanent' move from Kenley to Gravesend Airport adjacent to the Thames, close to the town of Gravesend. Whereas Kenley had been a regular RAF station with all the rigmarole like flagstaffs to hoist the Ensign up and so on, Gravesend was an impromptu airport wholly lacking in what one might term bullshit. This was the manner in which I much preferred to exist. That apart, I loved Gravesend because it was not shown on any of the Air Intelligence charts of the Luftwaffe; it couldn't have been because we were never bombed while I was there and we spent fifty-five halcyon days in this Dickensian area of Kent. Apart from a special flight whose role was to perform aerial reconnaissance of airborne German formations to fill in the gaps in the radar screen and those of the Royal Observer Corps, we were the only operational squadron based there. Jasper, I seem to remember, had to combine the duties of Squadron Commander with those of Camp Commandant – not that he had to do too much in the latter terms. In any case, he had an adjutant, an old chap with a RFC brevet, who could sort out the administration for him.

Another important appeal which Gravesend possessed was that in the clubhouse, which we used both as a pilots' room and a bar, there was also a piano which allowed Ken to do his stuff. *All the Things you Are, Stardust,* the gamut of Cole Porter, Irving Berlin and Jerome Kern used to emanate from that piano under Ken's artistry. But the nostalgia I feel about it was really due to a gramophone record someone picked up one day. We had a record player and we also had a tannoy broadcast system with speakers placed at strategic intervals around the airfield. The system was designed to allow the scramble order to be heard by everyone, ground crews and pilots; for this purpose, the microphone was positioned in the clubhouse and, of course, we used it to relay the scramble order to the ground-crews so they could get the propellers turning while we ran out to our Spitfires. (Funny thing that; why *run* when the immediate prospect is that you are going to meet your Maker? Why not walk?)

But the main function of the microphone in our case, by setting it alongside the gramophone, was to relay music all around the airfield. When this was combined with *Blue Orchids* – why it causes me even today to have twinges of awful nostalgia. *Blue Orchids* was never a smash hit, but to my mind it is the epitome of poetry in music. It is a very difficult tune to play, and although I made the attempt to learn it by heart – not being a straight-off reader of music on the piano – there are so many variations in the composition as to make it one of the most sophisticated melodies ever written. So it needs a competent pianist to do it justice. Nevertheless, *Blue Orchids* became our anthem. Before dawn simmered on the horizon the tune would have been broadcast around the air field. As night fell, we – or those of us who were still alive – would listen to it again.

> I dreamed of two blue orchids,
> Two wonderful blue orchids
> One night, when in my lonely room . . .
> But blue orchids only show in your eyes . . .

Tosh, maybe. But to me, sweet nostalgic tosh, still capable of bringing back memories of awful tragedies and, somehow, recollections of the happiest moments in my life. Jasper managed to find a gramophone record of *Blue Orchids* long after the war ended. He would sit, time after time, listening, until he burst into tears. Eventually his wife broke the record on his head. She could no longer stand such nostalgia which she could not comprehend. Wherever I went after the war, I would ask the local leader of the band if he knew the tune. Very few of them did, on account, no doubt, of the sheer difficulties in orchestration. So I gave up hope.

But twenty-five years after the Battle of Britain ended, I was staying in a hotel in Capetown, guzzling away at an enormous T-bone steak. The pianist was a woman and she was not only prolific in her artistry, she was also beautiful with her touch.

I wandered up to her.

'Like a drink?' I inquired.

'Wouldn't say no,' she replied.

I went to the bar and bought her drink, put it down on the top of the piano and with faint hope asked if she knew *Blue Orchids*.

' 'Course I know it,' she replied. 'It's my favourite melody.'

Then she played it to absolute perfection. I wept.

Ken should have been an Intelligence Officer; he had that sort of mind. One of his tricks was to get so close to a German aircraft as to be able to read the squadron letters; even the number. Poor old Ken; he did this once too often. It was, of course, valuable intelligence in that the general deployment of the units of the Luftwaffe was thus interpreted by British eyes and this was useful information. But one turbulent day Ken took off with his number two into a sky filled with cumulo-nimbus clouds, veritable thunderstorms were beating against the earth, and we never saw him again. He lost his number two on the climb in the thick clouds and we heard later that he had relayed by R/T the squadron letters and number of a Heinkel 111 to the controller. Then there was silence. Clearly he must have been flying in close formation on the German bomber to gain this information; in which case, machine-guns apart, the gunners could have killed him with their Mausers.

In those days, pilots were often overdue in terms of their expected time of landing, as some of them finished up in a field having belly-landed with a damaged aircraft and so on.

They would hardly make it their first priority to use the nearest telephone box to inform the squadron what was up, so we didn't worry unduly if a pilot was presumed missing until a decent interval of time had elapsed. Indeed, I was 'missing' for sufficient time on at least three occasions for the Air Ministry to have thought it necessary to signal my parents to that effect. But as the hours passed it became evident that Ken was indeed missing, and this was confirmed when his body was washed up out of the sea and his identity tag recognized for what it was. I had thought, somehow, that Ken was indestructible and I was proved wrong. Ken was not even in my flight but somehow his death hit me hardest of them all. Jasper sensed this, probably had a feeling of a kind of disintegration in the morale of one of his pilots, and was sharp of tongue over my reaction. Little did I know at the time that this was certainly the most severe blow he ever received in the whole of his life in emotional terms, because Ken was not only his personal pianist, so to speak: he was also his closest friend. Looking back over the years, it occurs to me that Jasper had the qualities of a great military commander, even if we kept the argument concentrated around the awful business of Ken's death. On the face of it he pressed on regardless, yet he was racked with grief but showed none of it. He had the Nelson touch all right.

It was about this time that I became Jasper's talisman. I don't know why, but he selected me to fly as his number two, on his right wing, for a particular sortie. The controller brought us up to immediate readiness in due course, but we stayed in the club-room which was only half a minute at a jog-trot from the line of Spitfires. Jasper was in charge of the poker school and I was playing chess with Happy Harpic when the telephone screeched. Twelve pairs of eyes bored holes in the back of the head of the airman who was manning the telephone and he knew it. But he was highly trained – he had to be. He waved his hand languorously above his head indicating that the message was not the scramble order. My knees unstiffened from the running posture and I continued to fix Happy via the chess board. He was a tall, thin, miserable Oxford don who was our Intelligence Officer, to me a very old man, then aged about 34, and I liked playing chess with him because I usually beat him.

The airman told Jasper that the controller wanted to talk to him and he strode to the telephone, heavy and burly with a glazed look in his eye. We all hated the telephone; the scramble order came over the telephone; I hate the telephone to this day. Jasper listened to what the controller had to tell him for only a few seconds, then he spoke into the receiver quietly but with icy venom.

'I don't bloody well want a weather report,' he said. 'I've already looked out of the window. It's going to be another bright blue day. Don't use this line again except for strictly operational purposes. Good-bye.'

Outside the glimmer of first light had extended into the breaking of dawn. The grass was wet with dew and the birds had only just begun to sing. I had not yet placed my parachute on to the wingtip because of the dampness in the air. Damp parachutes tend not to open when the handle is pulled, in which case one arrives at one's terminal velocity – at about 160 mph depending on various factors – before one makes a hole in the ground. I didn't particularly want this to happen to me. So my parachute was in my flying clothing locker.

I managed to get Happy screwed to the extent I would have check-mated him in another three moves when the telephone sounded again. This time, when I looked up, the airman's finger was describing a rotating movement meaning get the propellers turning – *Scramble!* Happy rose from his chair and knocked the chess board over with his knee.

'Sorry,' he lied. He knew when he was beaten.

Henry hastily removed *Blue Orchids* from the gramophone and bawled down the microphone '*Fibus Squadron Scramble!*'

I sidled towards my flying clothing locker amidst a crowd of swiftly moving bodies, hauled out my parachute – my flying helmet and gauntlets were already in the cockpit of LZ–X – and jog-trotted out to the Spitfire. Briggs held the parachute in position as I clamped the harness together and Jones, having started the engine, got out of the cockpit as I climbed on to the wing. Briggs heaved my backside and assisted me into the cockpit and I buckled down the safety straps. They uncoupled the starter battery. I set up the compass, gave the instrument a quick glance and waved my hand in front of my face. Jones and Briggs hauled the chocks away and I was ready to roll. I moved out of line and taxied carefully towards Jasper's Spitfire which was LZ–Y. When he moved out of the line I followed closely behind swinging the long nose of the Spitfire from side to side so as to see clearly ahead and not collide with starter batteries and the like. The Spitfire was a brute to taxi and it was imperative, therefore, to make a careful check of the pneumatic pressure gauge before attempting to move, as the brakes worked on air pressure; so did the guns, but the brakes had to be given priority attention while we were on the ground.

Gravesend was a grass airfield so we were fast reactors to the scramble order, whereas airfields with concrete runways and taxi-tracks meant that the fighters had to be taxied slowly for fear of colliding with one another, but slightly echeloned out, we could move at fair speed on the grass. Jasper got to the upwind end of the airfield, waited twenty seconds for the squadron to form up around him in long line abreast, put his hand above his head and dropped it, meaning he was opening his throttle for take-off. I did likewise and inched the throttle forward, playing the torque with my boots on the rudder-bars, and we gained speed bumping and lurching over the grass. Jasper retracted his undercarriage when he was about ten feet up and I followed suit. I retracted my radiator flap and adjusted the trims. Then I closed in tight on Jasper's right wing as we commenced the climb. When we were settled down, I skidded out to starboard and took a quick look at the squadron behind us. There were only eleven Spitfires; someone had failed to start his engine. I hoped he wouldn't be bloody fool enough to attempt to catch up with us on his own, or more likely than not the old reaper would cut his head off with his scythe in no time.

Jasper climbed to the North away from the raid, which was a good practice as the Messerschmitts could so easily bounce us while on the climb. I flicked my R/T transmitter button on and off again; the click told me it was working. Long transmissions were strictly out of court else the German Y service might have intercepted them and vectored the *Jagdgeshwader* on to us accordingly. Their freebooting sweeps were bad enough in any case without assistance from the Y Service, further to which they flew the flexible and loose finger-four formation whereas we flew like Fred Carno's circus.

The controller rang up.

'Fibus Leader. State your position.'

'Five miles north of Gravesend. Angels five. Still climbing.'

There was a pause.

'Understood. Inform when on interception course.'

The ROC had got us by now and we were a plaque on the controller's table in the Sector Ops Room. But this controller was good, very good. He didn't keep trying to vector us around like a swarm of bluebottles. I recognized his voice and could put a face to it. The face was burned from a fighter engagement in France earlier in the war. He was a good chap. Only fighter pilots should have been allowed to be controllers in those days. They understood the problems, they realized that they could not command a tactical battle, they appreciated that only a Squadron Commander could achieve that, they sensed that their duty was to provide a service, not to try to act like Napoleon at Austerlitz. They wouldn't try and get the squadron up sun and lunatic acts like that; they wouldn't demand this and that; they would simply give the Squadron Commander all the information at their disposal and leave him to sort out the mess.

Jasper climbed to about twenty thousand feet and then made a lazy wheel, turning us onto a southerly heading. He stayed just below the contrail layer so as to make us more or less invisible to the *Jagdgeshwader*. He was dead unlucky. We ran into the holocaust or, more properly, they bounced us. They must have been returning on course to meet up again with their French girlfriends and were up sun of us at that time of day. They still had enough petrol in their tanks to give us a rough time. Somebody yelled over the R/T *'Break'*, and Jasper wrapped around as he was by eleven fighters, had no other recourse but to haul back on the stick and stall-turn out of it. I was his Number Two and followed him up. A coupe of hundred feet below, as we wheeled over, I saw a Spitfire explode. It turned out to contain Henry: we would have to find another disc-jockey for our gramophone. All bloody hell was let loose and the situation became impossible to control. Jasper, quite rightly, decided to get the hell out. He flicked over on to his back and pulled into a vertical dive; I followed him – it is the job of a number two to keep pace with the leader no matter in which direction he prefers to fly. We fell like the autumn foliage from twenty-five thousand feet to ground level in no time at all. I stayed behind Jasper at about eight hundred yards. I thought he was going to hit the ground, but he suddenly went into a steep turn, just missing the ancient oaks of England by a few feet. I kept turning with him, still about eight hundred yards behind.

Then it occurred to me something might be amiss, so I called him up on the R/T

'Fibus Leader. This is Red Two. Are you in any difficulty?'

'Christ,' he said. 'I thought you were a bloody German!'

We flew back to Gravesend in a sedate manner and landed. Jasper heaved himself out of his cockpit and I joined him as he walked back to the clubhouse. Flight Sergeant Dennis intercepted us.

'Everything all right, sir?' he inquired.

'No,' Jasper snapped. 'Get all the bloody propeller spinners painted red as soon as possible.'

This was a good idea. One needed some distinctive form of identification in the sort of dog-fight we had just indulged in.

From that moment Jasper must have thought that I was an embryonic ace in that he had not managed to shake me off his tail on that sortie. So he appointed me as his permanent number two, his talisman, and as he flew on every possible sortie, and as he preferred not to fly unless I was alongside him, this meant that I had to fly on every possible sortie too. This had its advantages and disadvantages. On the one hand, being up with the Squadron Commander, who was normally the first to fire his guns, gave one greater opportunities to get right into the middle of the Luftwaffe. On the other, as Jasper had a stricter sense of duty than I did, one's social arrangements – if any – were occasionally placed awry. Like on the occasion when Jasper and I decided to have a day off, drive to London, do a bit of shopping, eat some oysters, drink a little and return. We hadn't even got to the Old Kent Road when the air-raid sirens began to wail. Jasper was driving the car and drew up at the kerb, got out and watched the contrails of a large formation of German aircraft overhead. He got back into the car, made a hairpin turn and drove on a reciprocal heading.

'What's the form, sir?' I inquired.

'Going back to the airfield,' he grunted. 'There's a bloody big raid.'

'But we haven't got a hope of getting at them,' I suggested. 'By the time we get to the airfield they'll all be sucking back claret in France.'

'Yes. But I've got a feeling they'll put in another bloody big raid later.'

It wasn't that Jasper did not have faith in the ability of his Senior Flight Commander whom he had left in charge during his temporary absence. It was merely that his sense of duty was of so high an order that he could not relax even for twelve hours.

And so it went on, day in day out. If only the weather had deteriorated that would have given us some respite. But the summer of 1940 was positively an Indian summer and September brought clear skies with hardly a speck of cloud. So we had to sweat it out. If the Luftwaffe took the decision to penetrate British air space, we had no recourse other than to obey the instructions of the controllers as they put us at readiness, or relaxed us to fifteen minutes readiness, or with luck thirty minutes readiness, or with great good fortune a period of stand-down. The casualty rate was appalling, and apart from the crudity of our methods, this was brought about by pilots arriving who could, so to speak, hardly ride a bicycle let alone take their Spitfires into action.

Shadowy figures came and went and one could see, not to be too dramatic, the look of death on the faces of some of them. We hadn't even got the time to give them a familiarization flight in the general area to learn where the important navigational pinpoints were. If a new chap survived his first half-dozen sorties he was dead lucky; if not he was dead anyway. There were, of course, natural fighter pilots who arrived on the squadron with reflexes sharp enough to survive, but these were the exceptions. In any case, it was not just the Luftwaffe one had to watch out for, it was occurrences such as the final act Johnny engaged in. We were on a battle climb and there was no sight of the Luftwaffe when Johnny's Spitfire imperceptibly began to bank away from the formation and then went into a dive, which became in all too short a course of time an almost vertical dive. I saw him go, broke formation and chased him down. He hadn't been shot at but there was quite clearly something wrong.

On the near vertical dive I tried to work out what had happened and came to the conclusion that, for whatever reason, his oxygen supply had failed. All I could think of to assist him was to call him up on the R/T. There was no reply. As the ground got dangerously close, I stopped calling him by his codename as used when in squadron formation and used his christian and then his surname. Nothing happened. His Spitfire continued in a near vertical dive at almost full throttle. I pulled out just in time to avoid striking terra firma a glancing blow, but Johnny didn't. His Spitfire exploded on impact with the ground and went on to form a very large crater. They dug Johnny out from under thirty feet of earth, or rather what was left of him which wasn't very much, placed his remains in a jampot, put it in a coffin and weighted the coffin with sandbags. Whereupon his parents arrived, having received the fatality signal, and requested that they be allowed a last look at their son. Fortunately, the officer in charge of the funeral tactfully pointed out that as the 'body' had had to be driven from A to B, it would be a rather unpleasant experience for them to see it in that condition. All they would have seen, in fact, was a jampot surrounded by sandbags.

FOUR

ARMAGEDDON

'MORNING, sir.'

I woke immediately. It was my batman, Williams, standing by my bed, mug of tea in his hand. The mug had a chip
on the rim; the tea was hot, sweet and very strong, whereas I
prefer weak China tea.

'What's the weather like?' I asked Williams. I had trained
him to be a good enough met. forecaster.

'It's going to be bloody awful, sir,' he said. 'It will be a
fine, blue day.'

If it had looked as if the cloud was going to be on the deck
he would have said a lovely day; and I could have gone on
sleeping. That didn't happen often in the summer of 1940.

He placed the mug on my bedside table.

'What's the date?' I asked.

'Don't know, sir. I'll have a look at the calendar in the
cleaning room and let you know.'

He exited. He was a sharp little Welshman, black hair
slicked, fond of the girls. He didn't have to press my clothes
or things like that as I scarcely wore anything except my
flying suit. His main duty was to look after my bull-terrier.
There was a strange affinity between the three of us – Williams, Crippen my dog, and me.

He came back.

'It's 15th September,' he said.

'Thanks.'

It didn't really matter whether it was 15th October. Time was meaningless. Days meant nothing. I wouldn't have known if it had been a Sunday or a Wednesday.

I sucked down the tea, crawled out of bed and shaved. Some chaps didn't bother to shave for the first sortie and that was none of my business. I preferred to shave. If the old reaper was going to swing his scythe in my direction I wanted my head to fall in the basket cleanshaven. I had a hand-propelled razor, apart from my electric one, and I had sometimes shaved on the battle climb. But the bristles kept falling into the oxygen mask and that could make for a dangerous situation. Compressed oxygen was my lifeline and I spent a lot of time breathing pure oxygen.

I threw off my pyjamas and dressed; this didn't take long. On top I had an RAF shirt with no collar attached. One turned the head with such frequency that a collar would have chafed the neck. Around my neck I wrapped the red silk scarf intended to alleviate the chafing, because the head was turned round so regularly to scan in the lethal area – a sector of about fifteen degrees dead astern. The rear-view mirror was helpful but only about sixty per cent effective. This left a forty per cent probability that one would be shot in the back before one saw the Germans coming in; that was an insufficient margin. It was up to me and no one else to ensure that I was among the right percentage; in this the scarf helped. It was also part and parcel of the aura of superstition in which we lived. It had been, in fact, the seventh veil of a seven veil dancer performing at the Empire theatre in Chatham. She had intended to remove only six of her scarves but I was waiting in the wings and was quicker than she. My action nearly brought the house down because she wasn't even wearing a G string. When I first put it round my neck it stank of cheap scent and perspiration and nearly gave me anoxia, but on the first sortie while wearing it I shot down two Messerschmitts – or thought I had. So it became my talisman, sharing the job with my Cornish pixie and LZ–X.

Finally, I pulled on my flying overalls which I had bought in London as the RAF issue was too cumbersome. I had the squadron badge sewn on the breast pocket which, in theory, for some outdated reason, was a breach of security in the terms that if I had forced landed in France the Germans would then know the identity of my squadron.

It was absolutely silent and calm as a sleeping baby as I walked out of the wooden shed which contained my bedroom. The grass was sopping wet with dew as I approached LZ–X and I walked on tiptoe to keep my socks dry; those thick woollen socks might have frozen up at thirty thousand feet if they were wet, with unfortunate implications. It was dark, black as a witch's heart, but I found my way to LZ–X by instinct and Jones and Briggs were there. Briggs was peering around the fuselage with a large torch looking for anything that might be unserviceable. Jones was about to get into the cockpit to run the engine up. The engine always had to be kept warm enough for an immediate scramble.

'I'll run her up, Jones,' I said.

He hesitated. He was aware that I knew nearly as much about the Merlin as he did, but not quite as much.

'I think I should be allowed to do that, sir,' he said. 'It is supposed to be my job.'

'OK. As you prefer. I'll come out later and do my own checks.'

He grinned with relief and clambered aboard LZ–X.

Jones was my age but Briggs was almost old enough to be my father. He held the rank of Aero-Mechanic which originated in the First World War. He could not write well enough to pass the exams which would have allowed him to remuster to a modern rank, so he could not make Corporal. But he was a first class rigger so I tried to fiddle the rules to get him the rank of Corporal without much success. It was not until I was appointed to command the squadron that I found out how to bend the rules; I then had him made Corporal and later Sergeant – which he well deserved. He had a face like a monkey's but his hands were full of artistry.

I wandered away from LZ–X to the dimly perceivable clubhouse at Gravesend Airport; first light had not yet begun to glimmer. The break of dawn was a good hour away. The lights were on behind the blackout screens in the clubhouse and Jasper was squatting by a blackboard making chalk marks in his thin handwriting. There were twelve crosses on the board representing Spitfires of the squadron in the crazy formation we used to fly, and alongside each Jasper was writing the names of the pilots detailed for the first sortie. I didn't have to look at the name of the formation leader because I knew Jasper would be in command – he normally was – and this meant that the name of his number two would be my own. Chris was to lead Yellow Section, the one immediately behind ours, and that was slightly worrying because although Chris had already been awarded the DFC and bar, he was suffering from nervous exhaustion and was, in my view, no longer reliable. But Bogle was to be one of the weavers if Jasper decided to put the weavers up as our lookouts, and that was good because Bogle was good; even better, Bogle was long-sighted. Apart from the section leaders and their number twos, some of the newly joined sediment had to be included in the formation although, naturally, Jasper would have much preferred to use only those pilots with adequate experience. But these boys had to get experience somehow or other and Jasper was not omnipotent and did not necessarily know who was going to be killed on any particular sortie, although I sometimes got flashes of inspiration about these things, if those are the right words to use.

I had not said 'good morning' or anything like that to

Jasper, as we had a tacit understanding that neither of us would talk to the other until dawn broke. Nor had I put *Blue Orchids* on the gramophone because the engine mechanics were running up the Merlins and no one would have heard the music except Jasper and myself. The rest of the squadron pilots began to enter the clubhouse, their faces were white with sleep; they wandered over to their flying lockers to sort out their helmets, gauntlets, parachutes and so forth. I took my accoutrements out of the locker and placed them strategically on a window ledge by the door. My flying goggles were strapped on to the flying helmet and I was particularly careful with them because they had cost me five pounds in Bond Street. The RAF issue types were wholly inadequate and mine were slightly tinted to give some assistance against the rays of the sun. Nor did they have rubber sockets to press around the eyes as rubber would burn quite well if one became a flamer, and whereas I never wanted to become a flamer, nor did I want to be blinded for the rest of my life, assuming I did manage to get out on the end of a parachute, because of inflammable rubber burning my eye sockets away.

When I reasoned that the air had dried out sufficiently, I heaved my parachute on my back and hauled it out to the Spitfire. First light had certainly materialized by now, but the birds were not sounding off and dawn had another half hour or so to wait. Jones was sitting in the cockpit of LZ–X with the cockpit lights glowing dimly. Briggs was nowhere to be seen, nor was there any need; he was probably swigging tea in the canteen. I shoved the parachute on to the wing-tip, harness hanging down. Some chaps preferred to place the parachute in the cockpit, but I thought I could get a quicker scramble time by having it on the wing-tip. One also had the safety harness to buckle up in the cockpit and this could lead to some confusion vis à vis the different straps.

Jones climbed out and I clambered into the cockpit. The

engine was warm enough for an immediate take-off, fore and aft trim was set correctly, the rudder trim needed correction, the pneumatic pressure was good and high so the brakes would work, and the gunsight was at brilliant and had to be turned down to dim. The firing button was on *Safe* and I wish it had been on *Safe* the day I nearly decapitated Briggs. This occurred when I landed after a frenzied sortie and forgot to turn the gun button from *Fire* to *Safe*. As I was beginning to undo my harness I pulled the stick back, the gun button struck my parachute buckle, eight Brownings fired simultaneously, and the stink of cordite was almost unbearable. Worse; Briggs was walking round the front of LZ–X to help me get out of the cockpit and his head was no more than one foot away from the outboard machine-gun when it burst into gun-fire. One more forward step and his head would have been blown off. The de Wilde bullets soared in a graceful arc into the skies of Kent and I watched their trajectory with blank amazement; but no farmers reported having any of their cows killed.

Briggs' face had turned green, but when the guns ceased firing he strode round the front of the Spitfire and clambered on to the wing. I saw his green face within inches of mine and it was covered with sweat.

'God, I'm sorry!' I said.

'Not to worry, sir,' he replied. 'But better put the bloody gun button on *Safe*.'

Which I hastily did.

When I got back to the clubhouse, rosy-fingered dawn, child of morning, was not very far away. But it was not quite Homer's milieu when I entered the room because Jasper was talking the nasal jargon of the East Side of New York *à la* Hadley Chase.

'Make wid de music,' he snarled, 'or I'll blow yer head off, you bum.'

'OK boss,' John replied, cowering as if he was about to be pistol-whipped, 'OK boss. Sure I'll make wid de music; sure boss I'll make wid de music.'

Jasper relaxed and John put the record of *Blue Orchids* on the gramophone turntable. The music sighed around the airfield and we got echoes which tended to conflict with the acoustics of the room. Jasper started up the poker school and Happy Harpic wandered up to me with the chess board. Then the cook appeared with a heavy metal container filled with big ugly sausages, fried eggs which resembled the eyes of a giant panda, and bacon. He placed the container on the hot plate and some chaps rose and helped themselves. I drew two mugs of tea from the urn, one for me and one for Happy Harpic. We began the game and I declined the queen's gambit because I knew that Happy inevitably got himself into a mess when this occurred. Then the telephone screeched, the airman rotated his finger, Happy did not even have to knock the chess board over with his knee as the game had only just begun.

There was always a sound and fury to a squadron scramble. There was a crackle of Merlins starting up and the roar as the propellers begin to rotate, dust blowing from behind the Spitfires, white smoke billowing from the exhaust stubs, airmen running, pilots jog-trotting, starter batteries being pulled out of harm's way, chocks being heaved away and pilots roaring their engines as they moved out of line. Briggs helped me to buckle on the parachute and Jones helped me to get the safety harness attached when I was in the cockpit. I set up the compass, checked that the pneumatic pressure was OK, oil pressure good and high, glycol temperature normal enough, waved the chocks away and moved out of line. I was senior enough now to have my own Spitfire and Jones and Briggs were in my permanent possession. These occasions in 1940 were the last days of the knight and his squires so to speak; we were a good team,

Jones, Briggs and myself, and I was about the fastest of them all to get my Spitfire moving for take-off.

I closed in on Jasper's starboard wing as we began to climb to the north.

'Fibus leader: one hundred plus crossing in at Dover, angels fifteen upwards,' the controller stated over the R/T.

'Understood,' Jasper replied. 'We are at angels fifteen, north of Gravesend, beginning a turn on to a southerly heading.'

'Understood. Vector one six zero. Make angels twenty-five.'

'Understood.'

I hung high above Jasper's Spitfire as we made a lazy turn to port. Below lay London, the Thames sweeping in serpent-like fashion through its very heart. The cement works on the Thames issued clouds of white smoke; the docks looked awfully empty. Then I saw Canterbury coming towards us with its great Gothic cathedral where Thomas à Beckett was murdered, which made me feel murderous towards the Teutonic gentlemen who were wrecking part of Britain's heritage with great regularity.

'Fibus leader. Squadron smoking,' came the voice of George.

'Understood,' Jasper replied. 'Losing height.'

He wanted to keep us out of the contrail area and remain relatively invisible to German eyes – and God knows there were enough such eyes peering in our direction.

We lost a bit of height and the controller vectored us towards the raid.

'Lose height to angels fifteen,' the controller requested.

He wanted to try and put us among the bombers. We went into a slow dive and we were now in battle formation.

'Bandits ahead – above and below,' came the voice of Pickles who had about the longest sight in the squadron.

65

'Understood,' Jasper replied. 'Am continuing to lose height.'

I saw nothing for about thirty seconds, then I saw black spots, which quickly transformed themselves into many bombers with fighters around them, and other fighters leaving tiny contrails high above. There must have been three hundred in the balbo and there were twelve of us. What was more they couldn't yet have been intercepted by any other squadrons as they seemed to be in cohesive formations. We were below them by now approaching them head on. I turned the gun-button on to *Fire*.

What Jasper thought he was doing I will never know, but it worked. He simply climbed the squadron into the middle of them. Incredibly, there were no mid-air collisions nor was there much time for me to do more than give them a couple of squirts with the Brownings. A German bomber whizzed past my head a few feet away. I could see the bomb-aimer in the perspex nose of the Heinkel. A few yards away a couple of Me 109s with dirty great yellow noses flashed past.

Then there was nothing, nothing at all. It is unbelievable how at one moment the sky can be filled with aircraft and then they all vanish. But I knew where they were going, so I hauled back on the stick and broke the seal on the throttle quadrant to gain maximum emergency power. The Merlin shuddered under the boost and black smoke streamed from the exhausts. I caught up with a Heinkel which was straggling; small wonder, as Jasper's unconventional attack had split the balbo up to no mean extent. I gained height on it and then throttled back on the dive in case the Merlin blew up through excessive boost. The de Wilde incendiaries hit the port engine a lucky strike I guess, and the engine blew up, whereupon the aircraft began to cart-wheel. I confirmed that it was a Heinkel 111 which meant that I had probably killed five men.

I gave the Merlin emergency boost once again and found

a Dornier 17. My bullets hit one of the engines and filthy black oil came back like a whiplash covering my windshield to the extent I could see nothing any longer through my gunsight. I half rolled out of it, got down to treetop level, opened my canopy and nursed the Merlin back to Gravesend. I made a three point landing with my head stuck out of the cockpit so I could see. The howl from the gunports as she stalled on to the ground, because the protective canvas had been shot away, informed Jones and Briggs that I had at least fired my guns in anger.

The squadron claimed twelve German aircraft destroyed on that sortie but how accurate those claims were I do not know. They had to be accurate for our Intelligence Officer, Happy Harpic, to pass them, so I assume it was a valid enough claim. I was probably the first to land, and Happy started to grill me; I told him what had happened.

'I'll grant you one confirmed for the Heinkel on fire,' he said primly, 'but I can only allow you one damaged for the Dornier.'

'Don't be a silly bugger,' I suggested. 'Sure I saw only one engine bust, then I couldn't see anything because my windshield was covered in oil. He could not possibly have returned home.'

'Sorry,' said Happy with a miserable grin on his thin lips. 'You've got to prove that you hit two engines, or saw the bandit spin in. Those are the rules.'

I climbed up on the wing and rubbed some oil off the windshield with my bare hand.

'Tell you what Happy,' I suggested, 'why not get this oil analysed so as to prove it was made in Germany, just in case you thought I put it there myself.'

'Oh, no. I trust you to that extent.'

Whereupon I rubbed the oil on his short-cut hair. He stank of oil for the next few weeks.

Jasper led the squadron into action on five occasions on

15th September 1940. Naturally enough, I was with him on his right wing each time.

On 11th October I was not flying in LZ–X – according to my pilot's logbook – but in another Spitfire, and I was leading a flight chasing some Me 109s, which were making their way in a haze of hundred octane fuel effluent in the general direction of France. We were faster than they, straight and level, but not all that much, so we were catching up only slowly.

We had crossed the coastline and I was about eight hundred yards behind a Me 109; I could even see the tail struts intrinsic to their design when a great sheet of oil from my engine suddenly splashed over my windshield and I could, of course, no longer see the Messerschmitt. At first I thought I must have been bounced by another German pilot but there was nothing to be seen in my mirror, so I hastily transferred my gaze to the instrument panel. The glycol temperature was already off the clock bringing in train the danger of imminent fire, the oil pressure showed *Nil* and the oil temperature was soaring beyond the bounds of prudence. So I switched off the two magnetos and the propeller sighed to a halt.

I put her into a long glide, opened the canopy which, fortunately, was not frozen up too thickly for the purpose, peered out and saw the coastline of England ahead; I had already instinctively turned on to a reciprocal heading. I calculated that I would arrive over somewhere like Folkestone at about five thousand feet as there was a tail wind, and I could either belly-land in a field or make for an airfield. I had the airscrew in coarse pitch to extend the glide and, sure enough, I crossed the English coast over Folkestone at about six thousand feet, whereupon British ack ack opened up on me, presumably in the belief that mine was a German aircraft. They missed me, of course, and I then saw Hawkinge airfield ahead. I put my undercarriage down when I was at about three thousand feet and turned, high and fast on to a final approach. I thereby made several grave errors of judgment. First, the pneumatic pressure on which my brakes depended was getting dangerously low as there was no engine running to maintain the pressure. Next, Hawkinge was a small grass airfield and the chances of achieving a successful landing from a glide approach were remote; I should never have put the undercart down. Finally, as I could see ahead only with my face stuck out of the cockpit, this increased difficulties.

I was fast as I crossed the threshold of the airfield, but it is better to be fast than to crash on an undershoot. I put the Spitfire down on three points half-way along the length of the airfield and applied full brakes. She tried to topple on to her nose so I released the brakes and she fell back on her tailwheel. The grass was damp and she had skidded in any case. I then gingerly applied the brakes again and nothing happened because I had run out of pneumatic pressure. I might have attempted to retact the undercarriage and drop her on her belly, but the barbed wire which enclosed the airfield boundary was by now looming up too fast. As it was obvious that I was going to run into the wire at about sixty mph I rested my gloved hand on the jagged gunsight and pressed my head firmly on my gauntleted hand so as to cushion the impact. She hit the wire hard, my head was thrust with great force on to my hand, she tried to cart-wheel forward and land on her back, but decided to stay with her tail-wheel high in the air.

I scrambled out in case she burst into flames, staggered out on to the grass and thought I deserved a swig of brandy. I always carried a flask filled with brandy in the left breast pocket of my flying overalls for occasions such as these. The fire engine came roaring out closely followed by an ambulance, by which time I had more or less emptied the flask of brandy and was blind drunk. An RAF car sped to the scene, overtook the fire engine and ambulance and a chap wearing a brass hat came over to me.

'Are you all right?' he said.

'Who the fucking hell are you?' I inquired.

'Take him to the sick quarters,' he told the ambulance crew.

It was the most extraordinary experience. I was so severely concussed that I completely lost my memory – but completely. I didn't even know that I was in the RAF, although what I thought I was doing in a small RAF hospital without being in that service did not occur to me as I was making no sense at all. Nor had the brandy done me any good, because strong drink when in a state of severe concussion makes for a situation of incompatibility.

I stayed in the sick-bay for a week and slowly, oh so slowly, bits and pieces of memory returned. But in due course I saw in my mind's eye the Messerschmitt; later I remember gliding over Folkestone; and when I could remember vividly that the gun-sight was on at strong brilliance when we hit the wire, I had more or less recovered.

'You shouldn't have drunk that brandy,' the doctor told me sternly as he signed my release papers. 'At first glance I thought you crashed because you were pissed out of your mind.'

'Any idea what happened to my aircraft?' I asked.

'Yes. The engineer officer told me they found a large chunk of British ack ack shell in the oil tank.'

I bet they were aiming at the Messerschmitts a couple of miles ahead of us – that would make for a two mile error which represented their average accuracy. But they also got Pickles who was flying in my formation. He tried to land somewhere near East Grinstead, ran out of airspeed and stalled into a small woodland. His Spitfire knocked down forty trees of some age and stature. All that was left of the wreck was Pickles and he was virtually unscathed. Pickles had the devil's luck, but Satan got him in the end.

Jasper sent a squadron car to pick me up. They had posted me as missing for the third time, and my mother was having another fit having received yet another telegram. When I arrived, Jasper said: 'Remember me?' 'I'll never forget you,' I replied. (Nor have I.)

He grinned. 'You forgot everything including me according to the medical reports I got from Hawkinge,' he said. 'Anyway, you've got to take sick-leave.'

'What on earth for?' I asked. 'I'm right as rain now.'

'Severe concussion and flying don't go together – according to the doctors,' he replied. 'So off you go.'

Reluctantly I climbed into the two-litre Lagonda which was my pride and joy and drove home. During my sick-leave my mother kept feeding me with orange juice and raw eggs for some extraordinary reason.

When I got back to Gravesend and the squadron, Jasper was no longer there. He had been promoted out of the job and posted. He left me a note.

Although I didn't appreciate it at the time, Jasper and I had a peculiar rapport which I have rarely experienced with other men. I have a host of acquaintances, a few hundred friends and about twenty men to whom I am deeply attached. How such affinity comes about, I do not know. Jasper was ten years older than myself and of a quite different disposition. His father was probably a parson, his grandfather almost certainly a dean. He did not conform in such vocational terms and I doubt if he was a religious man. He had a large head which contained a powerful intellect, but he preferred to conceal this. He inadvertently displayed his intellect by his obvious depth of knowledge of classical music. He was normally grim of face, which was an act of

71

deliberate deception and was occasionally exposed for what it was worth by the broad grin which tore away the iron mask. His laugh also found him out, and as he found some things amusing, he often laughed. It was more of a cackle than a laugh and he would expose his widely spaced, tobacco-stained teeth as he threw his head back like a stallion neighing.

Jasper was an inveterate gambler and punter. His obsession covered the roulette wheel, the card tables and the races. Long after the war ended, he would telephone me with the simple question 'heads or tails?'. If he lost, I would inevitably receive through the post a florin, the standard stake, contained in a crumpled-up piece of newspaper, representative of his integrity. His generosity was on an embarrassing scale and he would surreptitiously pay the waiter when I was unaware even when I had invited him out to dine. No force on earth would make him change his mind after he had effected such a subterfuge. I once infiltrated a five pound note into his pocket after he had paid my bill. He found it, dropped it on the floor and walked out. I had perforce to pick it up or leave it for the waiter to collect.

Jasper never showed any signs of fear, but this by no means implies that he was fearless; indeed, he was far too sensitive not to know fear. But whatever his inner feelings, he was on the face of it inevitably as calm as a statue of the Buddha. On one battle climb, for example, the controller rang up and informed him that a raid consisting of some three hundred bandits was crossing the coast in the Sandwich area. Having gained more intelligence, the controller then reported using the following words:

'Christ! I haven't seen reports on so many bandits since Michaelmas.'

'Understood,' Jasper replied, voice calm as a mother superior's confessing her sin to the local parish priest whose wellbeing depended entirely on her charity.

The controller then reported: 'I've made a quick calculation. There must be five hundred bandits crossing between Dover and Ramsgate. Good luck.'

'Understood,' Jasper replied, and then he addressed himself to the squadron. I wondered what he would do, what his executive order would be. I hoped he would order us to turn north and get the hell out of it. No such luck!

'Fibus Squadron,' he said over the R/T, 'we are just over-flying Lingfield racecourse. I wonder what won the two-thirty?'

He had the Nelson touch all right. We were comrades in arms which, I suspect, explains the deep and long-lasting affinity.

After his departure, I waited expectantly for the news of his having been awarded the DSO. He had led his squadron into action on every possible occasion. Under his leadership, in one fortnight alone, we had claimed over thirty German aircraft destroyed. He kept our morale at high pitch in desperate conditions and this needed a magician's cunning. Yet, in the event, he received not one award for gallantry, not even the DFC. My hatred for inept staff officers began at that time.

FIVE

REST-CURES AND WILDOATS

I HAD a very deep affection for and an attachment to Jasper, and instinctively resented the new Squadron Commander when I first met him – but not for long. Squadron Leader James Fisher must have been the man who acted as Ian Fleming's model when he created James Bond. James Fisher could do everything; he was sophisticated, a judo expert, God's gift to women together with an aquiline nose, he used a tailor in Savile Row both for his uniforms and civilian clothes, had a bootmaker in St. James's, his hair was cut with style, the nails on his strong artistic hands were well manicured, he was tough as an ox and he was one of the nicest men I have ever met. He used to break motor cars in head-on collisions with monotonous regularity. He was also a brilliant fighter pilot who, as a Flight Commander in another squadron, had been in the very thick of the Battle of Britain and turned out with a DFC and bar. Needless to say he was a completely different kettle of fish from Jasper, but I could never have had two more excellent men as my Squadron Commanders during my very impressionable years. Alongside James I was a comparative peasant.

James's first problem was who to appoint as a new Flight Commander because William had been promoted to take charge of another squadron. It was a nice decision to have to take because Bogle was in line for the job and had done better than I had during the Battle of Britain, and I was merely a month or two senior to him. According to the operational record Bogle should have got the job, but James felt that as I hadn't done badly, seniority must be the deciding factor so I was given the appointment. In any case, Bogle was promoted and posted to a flight in another squadron in short time, but, poor chap, he was killed in action not long afterwards.

An extraordinary policy was adopted at the end of October, 1940, when we were ordered to redeploy to West Malling which could have been only twenty miles away as the Spitfire flies from our well-beloved Gravesend. So the turmoil of another squadron move had to be undergone for no good reason whatsoever. Three of our Spitfires crashed when we landed at West Malling which was then a grass airfield. This was due to the fact that the Germans had bombed it quite heavily and some oaf of a civil engineer had filled up the craters with clay. The wheels of the Spitfires naturally sank into the clay after landing and toppled the aircraft on to their noses. The only good thing about West Malling was that we were the only squadron based there and the weather had set in in terms of a prolonged spell of misty conditions which meant we could not fly. So we went berserk instead. There were numerous trips to the delightful pubs in that area not far from Maidstone, and .38 revolvers were fired with great regularity from the cars as we sped home to our mess – not that we aimed at anything in particular or hit anything so far as I am aware. We stayed only one week at West Malling before some idiot in the planning department at Fighter Command Headquarters decided we would be better off at Biggin Hill, so another unnecessary movement order had to be written. By now we were equipped with Spitfires Mark Two, which had a better performance than the Mark One, but I hung on to the letters LZ–X for my personal aircraft.

The weather at Biggin really clamped down for a very long period and I doubt if we took to the air to any extent over a period of some six weeks; so we went further berserk. There were two other squadrons at Biggin and we thought as little of them as they did of us. The officers in one of the squadrons were highly sophisticated and were billeted not far from the airfield in a country house which had been requisitioned over its owners' heads. If the owners had ever known what went on in that house, they would probably have sued the Air Ministry for a large sum of money as reparation. These boys really lived it up. For a start they all owned or shared in a fleet of Cadillacs, they had their own dance-band made up from those ground personnel of the squadron who could play the piano, or the trumpet, or the clarinet; there was one chap who could even play the harp. It was, in fact, an extremely good dance band. Then they had their women who lived with them in the house, and some gorgeous floozies were available there for inspection. They hired a London catering firm to provide their food and wine and they lived like princes. Despite this profligate way of living they weren't too bad operationally, although they did lose nineteen Spitfires destroyed or damaged in a single fortnight against their claims of sixteen German aircraft destroyed.

The other squadron was completely differently organized and was under the command of the redoubtable South African ace, Sailor Malan. He made his pilots live by comparison like Boer farmers in their wagons. He even made sure that they went to bed at ten p.m. each night although, presumably, he did not actually close their eyelids for them. He was tough, strict, a martinent and operationally it paid off. I doubt if there was a more successful Squadron Commander in 1940 than Malan. He had been a merchant seaman – hence his nickname 'Sailor'. He was so long-sighted he could have seen a fly on the Great Wall of China at five miles. He was a crack shot, a brilliant aerobatic pilot, but above all he was utterly determined. He even won a dog-fight against the redoubtable German fighter ace, Mölders, who finished the war with well over a hundred kills. If Malan had had decent enough armament instead of the puny battery of eight ·303 in. Brownings we were equipped with, Mölders would never have got back to his base at Wissant; he would have been dead as mutton. But I could never have survived under Sailor Malan's command. His outlook and mine on life were so completely opposed as to make the whole thing too incompatible to make any sense at all.

Then the Secretary of State for Air paid a visit, and James – who could have made his fortune as a con-man and prob-ably has by now – took him on one side.

'We have problems, sir,' he stated.

'Tell me how I can assist,' said Sir Archibald Sinclair.

James got brocaded curtains for our dispersal hut, in-creased the establishment of ground personnel in the squadron by a third, and the next day there were delivered three large Ford shooting brakes with V 8 engines, each capable of containing nine pilots in normal conditions or fifteen if there was a party to go to. James decided, as there was hardly any flying going on, that we should make the West End of London our Mecca. Each evening, accordingly, three large Ford shooting brakes would whizz up in convoy to such diverse establishments as the Dorchester, the Grosvenor House, the Mayfair and some odd little places in Soho that James knew well. The experience made even me quite a sophisticated chap. We had to wear uniforms at that stage of the war, whenever we went to places as diverse as Dickensian pubs in Kent, or the Dorchester in London. By this time we were recognizable as part of the gang which comprised Winston Churchill's 'few' and we were adulated, although the bombs were dropping with great frequency on

London by night meaning that we had not really defeated the Luftwaffe after all.

Perhaps I had better expand on this. It is all too easy to believe, especially if you were personally involved, that Fighter Command won a great victory over the Luftwaffe in 1940. Certainly the pilots of Fighter Command destroyed more German aircraft than we lost, but given adequate planning in the pre-war years and a more competent handling of the fighter force in 1940, the Battle of Britain could have turned out to be a disaster for the Luftwaffe. In the fortnight ended 6th September, however, Fighter Command lost 103 pilots killed and 128 seriously wounded, and 466 Spitfires and Hurricanes were destroyed or seriously damaged. There was really no need for such slaughter had the Air Marshals displayed any military nous between 1931 and 1940. As a matter of historical fact, Eleven Group lost control over the air situation on about 1st September and the Luftwaffe could have covered the amphibious invasion – if Operation Sealion had ever been militarily feasible. In the event the Luftwaffe was by no means a defeated force, although its aircrews were certainly disheartened. However, London was bombed on fifty-five consecutive nights from 7th September onwards, and a great number of British cities suffered to a greater or lesser degree. So clearly the Luftwaffe was not defeated by Fighter Command on 15th September, 1940, and, indeed, penetrations as far as London were continued for weeks after by the use of fighter-bombers. But we had better not enter the lists of aerial strategy in a book of this kind.

Nevertheless it was a pleasant experience to be fêted whether we deserved it or not, made the more so when, on one occasion, in some night-joint or other, a waiter came up and placed six bottles of champagne in ice buckets on our table.

'I didn't order that,' James said with horror.

78

'With the compliments of one of our members, sir,' the waiter replied.

I found out that he was a Jew. I am not anti-Semitic and I was even more inclined to assume that Balfour's declaration was an excellent document when I had finished my ration of Jewish donated champagne. One night when the convoy assembled for the drive back to Biggin, the bombs were beginning to drop. Earth-shaking blasts put the Fords on to two wheels; showers of incendiary bombs kept igniting all around us; I saw two factories begin to blaze. James's reaction was to increase the speed of our convoy through the streets of London from sixty mph to eighty; even the police cars couldn't keep up with us. But, somehow, we got back in one piece. It was great fun; one was, after all, still not long out of school. Further, one was so drunk that a near-fatal car crash would have caused no pain at all.

Then the weather broke – to our disadvantage socially – and we were in the air again. We changed our tactics – very belatedly let it be said – from interception patrols to readiness patrols. This meant that instead of being at readiness on the ground, we flew combat patrols on a line such as, for example, one lying between Canterbury and Dover. This paid off on, for instance, 14th November, 1940, when, for some extraordinary reason, Kesselring decided to take some of his Ju 87s out of their cocoons and ordered them into an attack on Dover Harbour. We were flying on a readiness patrol and were somewhere in the area of Maidstone on a southerly heading when the controller rang James up on the R/T.

'Bandits, fifty plus, heading for Dover.'

'Understood,' James replied. 'Fibus squadron – *Buster!*'

This was the Codeword which meant full boost, break the seals on the throttle quadrant, get a move on. I naturally broke my seal else I would have lost James in a haze of a hundred octane effluent. We got to Dover quicker than a smash and grab raider gets away with the loot from a shop in Bond Street. There were some fifty Ju 87s just starting their dive bombing attacks, covered by about fifty Me 109s. The Ju 87 had air brakes to assist it in maintaining a vertical dive without exceeding the speed in terms of the design limits of the aircraft. We had no such facility and could not, therefore, dive after them vertically for any length of time, and in any case we would have overshot them. So we went into a lazy dive, ignored the Me 109s who were in a difficult predicament anyway, as another squadron was engaging them, and then shell bursts from British ack ack started to appear in the area not only of the Ju 87s but also ourselves who were gently catching up with them. They missed the Ju 87s needless to say, but I was struck a glancing blow and my flying boots were punctured, leaving pieces of metal in my legs. But the flight instruments were OK so I pulled out of the dive when the 87s did, and made an astern attack on one which then began to burn. The 87 had only one rear gunner with one machine-gun and was extremely vulnerable; nor could they cruise at much more than 150 mph. I shot at least four 87s and on the final attack when my ammunition ran out, my target dropped into the sea with a horrific explosion. I could claim two German aircraft destroyed but Happy credited me with only one destroyed, one possible and two damaged. I think he was miles out in his appreciation – but what did it matter?

On the night of 14th November, the same day as this incident related above, the Luftwaffe's bombers made a scorching attack on the ancient city of Coventry and, among other things, destroyed the fourteenth-century cathedral. I expect I killed six or more members of the Luftwaffe earlier that day.

So what?

A week later, I was leading the squadron on an operational scramble when my number four rang up on the R/T and said he had lost sight of the squadron. I remembered the voice and recognized it as belonging to a newly joined Sergeant Pilot; I told him I was at fifteen thousand feet climbing to twenty-five thousand feet into the sun and would he bloody well catch up, but fast. He took me too literally and was obviously blinded by the sun. For the next thing I knew was that the airframe of a Spitfire struck the nose cowling of mine, tore my propeller off and there was on the one hand the screech of a Merlin revving far beyond its design limits, on the other the crunch of duralumin being torn into shreds, combined with a dangerous loss of control as the stick tended to jump around the cockpit. I remember seeing the Sergeant Pilot's Spitfire diving away vertically and took note that it no longer possessed either elevators or a tailfin. He would never get out of that, whereas I could just about get out of LZ–X – provided I could open the canopy. They had, in fact, recently provided a modification, which, as far as the pilot was concerned, meant that if one pulled a black rubber ball just above one's head, the canopy, in theory, would jettison.

Hopefully, I pulled the rubber knob and, sure enough, the canopy vanished into thin air leaving behind a literal hurricane as the air was sucked into the cockpit at some 250 mph. It even made my cheeks expand like a balloon until I closed my mouth. I released the oxygen tube, unclipped the harness, clambered up until I was standing on the cockpit seat and then the wind blew me out of LZ–X. The tail end of the Spitfire missed my head by no more than two feet, which was fortunate. I had made several grave errors of judgement in getting out but, on the other hand, I was in rather a hurry. I don't remember having pulled the ripcord of the parachute, but the next thing I knew was that its canopy was open above my head and I was, seemingly, stationary in mid-air at about ten thousand feet. There was complete silence as I watched my Spitfire dive to its grave and burst into flames when it hit the ground. I hoped that it hadn't landed on somebody (nor did it in fact).

Then my intrinsic love for the air really materialized. There was just me and the air, and we appeared to be clinging to each other, apparently for ever and ever amen. Indeed, at one moment, it occurred to me that I was a ghost, a soul half-way to limbo. The enchanted mutterings and babbling gossip of the air relaxed my nervous tension. An ancient Greek poet once wrote that the old age of an eagle was better than the youth of a sparrow. I was getting older every second; I quite agreed with him. Let me lap in soft Lydian air high above the smoke of what men call earth. No longer did the air seem to me to be a foul and pestilential complex of vapours, more like a majestic roof fretted with golden fire, more like a most excellent canopy. But this was only because the canopy of my parachute was firmly and bravely allowing me to descend with the utmost gentleness to that quintessence of dust called Earth. There I was crawling between heaven and earth, and as I slowly descended, I thought of little English churches, curates long dust coming and going on lissom toe. Above were the blue-massing clouds; my lust for fame was just a dream; suns and universes ceased to be; I saw heaven's glories shine – sure I did. It was ephemeral, it was transient, it was transcendent, it was a fleeting view of heaven.

Having hung in mid-air for what seemed to be infinity, there was suddenly the ground coming up – fast. Worse: there was a line of pylons which must have meant that high-voltage electricity cables would be hung on to them and, or so it seemed to me, there was no possibility of avoidance. No one had taught me the intricacies of how to take avoiding action when on the end of a parachute, but the situation was becoming more desperate every second. So I lurched to one side and spilled the air from out of the parachute canopy simultaneously. I nearly went into a kind of spin. However, this was good enough to change my direction; I was now clear of the electricity cables and was obviously going to fall through the foliage of an ancient English oak which someone had planted there over four hundred years ago.

My boots went into the foliage with an appalling crash and tearing noises, and quite large chunks of branches fell to the ground as my body assisted in the process of destruction. I put my hands over my face to avoid my eyes being gouged out by the branches, and then jerked to a sudden halt as the parachute canopy became finally engaged with the topmost branches; and I dangled like a yoyo about thirty feet from the ground but about ten feet away from the tree-trunk itself. I swung there like a hypnotist's watch for about five minutes wondering how in Heaven's name I could get down to ground level. Then I remembered my father's clock and its pendulum, began to heave my body to and fro. I gained impetus, and was at one moment almost clutching the thick trunk of the tree, twenty feet away from it the next. I seized my fleeting opportunity and snatched hold of the trunk, grabbing at the thick bark with my fingernails. The tree was greasy and had a strong smell after the pure air I had recently been breathing. I clung to the tree, looked down and saw a thick branch a few feet below my boots, decided to unbuckle my parachute and then scrambled down to the branch. By making use of other branches it was comparatively easy to get down nearly to ground level, but finally I had to drop ten feet to hit the ground as I had then run out of branches.

I fell with a resounding thump and was temporarily dazed, but when my brain cleared I took note that I was surrounded by a small posse of old men with pitch-forks in their hands, and then I spotted one with an ancient 12 bore shot-gun which was pointed at my head.

'*Donner und blitzen,*' he said menacingly.

'Piss off, you stupid old bastard,' I replied.

He lowered his shot-gun with obvious disappointment.

'Gurny,' he said, 'this one's a bloody Englishman.'

'Course I'm a bloody Englishman,' I told him. 'Do I look like a bloody Hun?'

'Now you come to say so, sir,' he replied, 'I don't think you do. But, you know, us in the Home Guard 'ave got to take proper precautions. Any case you can't go anywhere 'til the Army identifies you proper like.'

Then there arrived an officious Army officer in a car with a Corporal.

The Home Guard platoon explained their suspicions that I must be English but he eyed me with distaste.

'You'd better come with me,' he said in a clipped military voice. 'We've got an interrogation centre in East Grinstead. I can't release you until your identity has been confirmed.'

I had already had a very long morning, so I kicked him on the shin.

'Ooch!' he shrieked, head lowered in agony.

At that moment, a car arrived with some intelligent people aboard, sized up the situation, told the Army officer to stop playing soldiers. They, they said, would vouch for me and I would be available in their nearby house. Would he telephone the nearest RAF station and have a car sent down to their address. He could do nothing except comply; they were well known in the district. She was the wife of a whisky magnate and had her daughter and prospective son-in-law with her. Almost everyone in East Grinstead had seen me floating down like part of the autumn foliage on the end of my parachute, and they had nothing much better to do because it was a calm Sunday morning and the pubs were not yet open.

She gave me a stiff whisky, and as I now knew who she was, I was amused to note that she didn't have the same brand in her house as her husband's distillery made. She asked me to sign her visitors book and suggested that I put down my address as 'From Heaven' which I did. An RAF car drew up outside, I thanked my hostess and departed, having first told the disgruntled Army officer, who was still wondering whether I had broken his leg with my boot or not, that it would be a useful training exercise if he arranged for my parachute to be taken out of the tree and dispatched to an appropriate RAF unit. I hope I did break his leg.

We were kept reasonably busy at Biggin Hill and the old year disappeared from the calendar and 1941 turned up. We were scrambled one day and I was leading the squadron on an operational sortie as James had quite reasonably decided to take a day off in London, and Harry, the senior Flight Commander, was half-way across the English Channel on a radar calibration flight. There was a layer of alto-cumulus cloud which I estimated to be about three thousand feet thick with its base at approximately fifteen thousand feet.

'Penetrate cloud on a vector of one eight zero,' the controller said. 'Bandits of the fighter type will be about ten miles south of you proceeding on a northerly heading when you break cloud.'

This was one of those armchair Napoleons all right, and I brooded over the information he had given me. I sensed it was spurious, but I didn't know what other squadrons he might have had directed on to the same raid under control, so I reluctantly concluded that he must know what he was about. I was quite mistaken – he hadn't got the first idea. I told the chaps to get into close formation and climbed into the cloud; I put them into battle formation after the blinding glare of the sun hit us as we surged upwards from the grey of the cloud. Then somebody screamed over the R/T *'Break!'*

We broke and there were about fifty Me 109s diving at us.

'Jack it round, jack it round!' somebody said over the R/T, and I vaguely wondered who was supposed to jack it round.

Then there was a very loud bang in my cockpit followed by the stink of explosives, my right arm was hurtled into the air, and my gauntleted hand hit the cockpit canopy with such force as to bruise the knuckles very severely, as I later discovered. I gave her full boost and transferred my left hand to the control column as the right arm was now hanging helplessly down at my side, and jacked her round as hard as I could turn. The Spitfire could out-turn the Me 109 at medium altitudes and I got on to his tail. He had a big yellow nose and he had two 20 mm cannon in his wings. I closed to within 250 yards range and pressed the firing button. He was a dead duck. But nothing happened. I glanced at the pneumatic pressure gauge and saw it was reading empty. He had hit my air bottle. I half rolled out and escaped into cloud. Then I set course for Biggin Hill at low level. I had thought of ramming him but wondered whether I could have baled out in time if I had taken such action. That would not have been possible, I discovered, when I attempted to open my cockpit canopy which was jammed firmly shut.

When I arrived over the airfield, I joined circuit, switched on my navigation lights in the optimistic hope that they were still working as some indication to others that I was in trouble – my R/T set had also been blown up. Some half-witted pilot drew into formation with me on the circuit and indicated that my navigation lights were alight. I was in no position to remove my left hand from the control-column to give him a rude message.

There was a squadron of Spitfires lined up on the shorter of the two runways ready to roll for take-off. I needed the longer runway and touched down across their take-off path just as the leading section almost arrived where I was. A few seconds and they would have cut my head off whilst on their take-off run. I lowered the undercarriage via emergency air and she ran on down the runway but the brakes wouldn't work because the pneumatic system was smashed. I ruddered her hard when I arrived at the end of the runway, to keep away from the barbed-wire, and gave her a burst of throttle to assist the turning process. She bumbled over the grass heading straight for the squadron dispersal hut. A half-witted airman began to give me signals in the belief that I was making a normal, if somewhat unconventional, return to the squadron line. As I was still doing at least twenty mph he realized the error of his ways, ran like a hare and got the hell out of it.

It was by now pretty obvious that I was going to take the squadron dispersal hut down; the ground crews made the same appreciation and removed themselves. Then, fortunately, my wheels struck a filled-in bomb crater, the Spitfire banged up on to her nose, thought for a moment whether she would cartwheel on to her back, decided not to, and stayed with her tail in the air. They had to get a jemmy to break open the cockpit canopy as two German bullets had hit the runners. I could never have baled out if I had rammed him. They found forty bullet holes in LZ–X and another one caused by a cannon shell.

They took me to Guys Hospital which was then dispersed to Orpington and an Indian surgeon performed an immaculate operation to remove chunks of lead from my arm; he had to work under X-ray conditions as some pieces were very small and too near the ulna nerve for comfort. If they had shifted in the course of time and affected the ulna, they would have paralysed my fingers.

I came to, having been under a general anaesthetic for four hours and there was a very attractive nurse by my side.

'Feel my pulse nurse,' I suggested lecherously, 'just in case I'm going to die.'

87

'You're not going to die,' she said, 'and in any case I've been feeling your pulse for the last few hours, so I'm fed up with feeling your pulse.'

She was quite a dish.

They then decided we had seen enough action for the time being and that the squadron needed a rest from operations. So James flew the squadron off on a westerly heading and I found another pilot available to drive me down in the Lagonda as my arm was still in a sling and I couldn't drive. He kept crashing the gears, much to my fury, although there were admittedly quite a few tricks one had to learn to make a clean change of gears in that car. My batman, Williams, thought he needed a rest from his operation of looking after me and my bull-terrier, so he applied for leave and was given three weeks time off, which he richly deserved. So I needed a temporary batman and they gave me a batwoman instead. At first, I thought this to be rather infra dig, like losing one's butler and being given a parlour maid in lieu. Then I appreciated that this might have its advantages, because they gave me the services of Gertie.

Gertie was about eighteen years of age, with natural blonde hair, beautiful blue eyes and lascivious lips. Her uplift was of sufficient weight without being too vulgar, and she had trim ankles and good legs. Her chore was to give me tea in the morning, press my clothes, stoke up the coke stove which kept the room warm, look after my dog and so forth. My arm was not yet strong enough to pilot a Spitfire and I looked after the office work and generally mooched around.

I think Gertie and I came to a similar conclusion at about the same moment in time. I would lie on my bed of an evening gazing with fascination at her trim backside as she heaved coke into the stove. She used to bring me cocoa before she retired and it began to dawn on me that the buttons on her shirt were all tending to fall away. First there was one missing, the next night there were two, later the third and fourth buttons were hanging on by merely a thread. When it became obvious that the weight of her uplift had increased considerably, it occurred to me that she had taken to not wearing a brassiere. It followed that Gertie had one special shirt for me, with the buttons missing, and others which she wore for the purpose of going on parade. She didn't wear a tunic for my household chores, merely a blue RAF shirt, a skirt and so on. By now I was getting glimpses of her cleavage – and how!

One evening, as she was stoking up the fire, her backside fascinated me more than usual and when she later leaned over me to put the cocoa by my bedside table, she had only one button retained on her shirt, and that was about to drop off under the weight of her uplift. So I came to a decision.

'Gertie,' I inquired, 'can I help you at all? My arm is much better now.'

'No thank you, sir,' she replied, 'anyway I've stoked up the stove for the night.'

'Have you had your evening meal in the mess?' I asked her.

'Yes, sir, I have indeed.'

'Well, Gertie,' I said, 'what I meant when I asked if I could assist, was can I help you get your knickers down?'

'No need for that, sir,' she giggled. 'I don't wear any, anyhow.'

Whereupon she drew her skirt high above her head to prove it. Nor did she wear any knickers.

Gertie and I had a fine old time. I was frustrated when Williams returned from leave. I didn't learn about women from the Colonel's lady or Judy O'Grady; I learned about women from Gertie!

Then they decided to move us even further west, to

Cornwall, where our major role was supposed to be that of maintaining standing patrols over coastal convoys. This would have been deadly boring if we had not been billeted in a decent hotel overlooking the tumultuous Cornish seas, which represented our mess. The squadron officers were given the top floor in its entirety for their rooms, whereas the two floors below were still available for holiday-makers. As our reputation spread, it became fairly obvious that the hotel was booked up well ahead for the summer of 1941, by London female secretaries and the like, who demanded bedrooms on the second floor just below the one which contained our bedrooms. This must have been because the fornication we indulged in was on a massive scale and the news spread abroad. Why, the walls of the hotel used practically to shake due to our combined efforts.

The girls usually stayed for only one week, and those of us who were not on flying duty on Saturday mornings, would sit on the steps of the hotel watching the booty arrive from the Cornish Riviera Express. James, through sheer force of seniority, was allowed the pick of the litter but I, by now being fairly senior, got about second best. They came in all shapes and sizes, tall ones, short ones, fat ones, skinny ones; those with enormous uplift, those with bosoms weighing not too much, and those with a breast development akin to that of a boy. There were blondes, brunettes, red heads, titians, auburns, mouse coloured and brown heads. There was an unwritten law that when a chap had been granted his selection, no other pilot could take over the tenancy, so to speak. Gertie had given me the taste for sexual licentiousness, and Gertie was a lovable creature and I am grateful to her even to this day – although God only knows what she is up to nowadays.

Without any question at all, James was the most successful wooer and usually achieved his objective a couple of days ahead of me. This handsome, elegant, sophisticated, gallant man could have pinched Nell Gwynne from good King Charles in no time at all. In fact, in a previous incarnation, I expect he did. He would take his selected number down to the local five star hotel, fill her up with good food and champagne, and she would then crumble quicker than a rat running away from a bull-terrier. I was rather more modest in my form of wooing but I never had a failure, which wasn't bad considering my relative inexperience compared with that of James who had been at the game for at least ten years longer than I had.

I used to swop around my style of girls; on one week deliberately selecting a fat one, for example, whereas the previous week I had concentrated on a thin one. I even went in for changes of hair colouring. We were so discreet that the hotel proprietor only had a sneaking suspicion of what we were getting up to; but he must have wondered why great cracks kept appearing in his walls – which was due to the silent reverberations brought about by the sheer scale of our activities. Love, at this period, never entered my head: I was only there, so to speak, for the fornication. But not only did we enjoy this pleasant little interlude: so did the girls. Almost to a woman they returned to the trials and tribulations of living in London during the war, refreshed in mind and sullied in body. In any case, they must have enjoyed themselves because they obviously told their girlfriends all about this haven in Cornwall.

'You get there, Mabel,' they probably said, 'and you find a glamorous bunch of fighter pilots sitting on the steps. If you are extremely lucky and get the senior one, the squadron commander whose name is James, he gives you champagne first. If you're not so lucky you get a chap called Dizzy who gives you beer. Then you go on down the scale; but whoever you get is good from all accounts.'

'Ooh,' the various Mabels would probably reply, tightening up their loins before rushing off to Paddington to buy a ticket on the Cornish Riviera Express. At least, that's the way it seemed to work. The hotel proprietor must have made a fortune in the summer of 1941. His rooms were booked in advance to the 100 per cent mark. *Gloria Finis!* (which means it is a glorious way to die!).

SIX

SQUADRON COMMANDER

THEY gave us Spitfires with a long range tank and a cruder device would be hard to imagine. The 'long range' ability was built in by constructing a fat ugly petrol tank under one wing which contained an extra thirty gallons of petrol. This caused the aircraft to yaw quite violently on take-off, made for a dangerous situation if one had to belly-land, and in any case was designed purely for the purpose of extending the ferry range, never originally intended to be utilized on operations; on operations it naturally increased one's vulnerability. But one of the bunch of maniacs in the Air Ministry, or in Fighter Command Headquarters, was probably awarded an OBE for having a good idea which, in effect, put the lives of the squadron pilots involved in greater jeopardy than before. The Air Staff first decided to use these Spitfires for long range escort work, then changed their minds and gave us cannon-equipped Spitfires of a more modern mark. But, they said, we must not fire our cannon except against German aircraft as there were insufficient supplies of 20 mm cannon shells for gunnery practice. We didn't see any of the members of the Luftwaffe for about a month, so I came to the conclusion that perhaps we ought to test these cannon just to get the feel of things. The recoil forces involved in firing cannon, in fact, reduced the speed for the aircraft by some thirty mph which was an operational factor of considerable importance. (This, at that time, we did not know.)

One day I rang up the Station Armament Officer at the major sector airfield a few miles away and told him that I was going to take off shortly and test the cannon.

'You can't do that!' he exclaimed. 'You will be in breach of specific orders laid down by Group Headquarters.'

'Hard luck,' I replied. 'I'll give you a report in due course.'

I found a rock about thirty miles from the Cornish coast, dived at it and pressed the firing button. One cannon shell emerged from each gun and they then both jammed solid. Seagulls flew from the rock as the two shells made impact. I landed back at the airfield, took up another Spitfire and tried again. Exactly the same thing happened. We had been flying on operations for some considerable time with no effective armament. Our Squadron Armament NCO then had a chance to evaluate the cannon and found everything that could be wrong was at fault in the machining of the cannon. I gave the Station Armament Officer a report and within two days our 'cannon firing' Spitfires were removed and we were given back the old long range horrors with merely eight Brownings. This was pathetic staff work amounting, indeed, to criminal negligence.

But as there was in existence a small force of Spitfires which quite fortuitously contained thirty gallons more fuel than normal, it was felt by the policy makers that use must be made of them operationally even though the extra tank was never intended for operational purposes. The top brass got over-excited at the vision projected, that three squadrons of Spitfires which carried thirty additional gallons of fuel – two other unfortunate squadrons were similarly equipped – was a war-winning system. So a plan was formulated whereby the available force of Blenheim bombers, with us as their fighter escort, should be used, day in day out, against enemy coastal convoys plying to places like Rotterdam. Accordingly, we were constantly ordered to re-deploy from Cornwall on a temporary basis to airfields in East Anglia where our task the next morning would be to rendezvous with a force of Blenheims and escort them to the coast of Holland over the North Sea and, hopefully, back again.

This was crazy planning on the part of the Air Staff. The Blenheim, for example, was useless as a military aircraft although the fighter version did have a capability as an embryonic night fighter. Our Spitfires were primitive in the terms of the day and most of them had flown too many hours for safety, let alone operational performance. We had been heavily out-gunned during the Battle of Britain and by now the remainder of the force in Fighter Command was equipped with cannon firing Spitfires which actually worked. We, on the other hand, flying at the extremity of our range, had to rely on batteries of eight .303in Brownings. Our only possible recourse, rather as in the case of the charge of the Light Brigade, was not to reason why but to do our best.

Notwithstanding, time out of mind we would take off from airfields in East Anglia, pick up a squadron of Blenheims and then split up according to plan. Six Blenheims would head that way and the other six thither. Simultaneously we would break up our squadron formation and one of our flights would escort one formation of Blenheims and the second flight would stay with the other. We would fly for a hundred miles or so until we saw the Dutch coast ahead, then the Blenheim leader would make a sweep searching for coastal convoys. If and when the formation leader spotted a convoy, which occurred with great regularity, he would dive low over the water together with his formation; we would keep slightly above and watch out for intercepting German fighters. By this time, of course, the

Germans had placed flak ships fitted with lethal anti-aircraft guns in the convoys. Had the Blenheims been fitted with aerial torpedoes, there might have been some sense in the operation as they could have released their torpedoes, turned away out of range of the flak barrage and possibly survived. But as it was, they were equipped only with 500 lb bombs which meant they had to overfly the convoys and also the deadly flak ships.

It was no part of our role to enter the flak barrage; we were a purely anti-fighter escorting force. Consequently, as the Blenheims went in for their final bombing run, we would fly around the convoys with the aim of giving protection to the Blenheims again when they had passed over the barrage. But the trouble was that all too few Blenheims managed to survive the flak. In my estimation, on every sortie I undertook when I had the responsibility of escorting six Blenheims, four were normally destroyed by flak. On not one occasion did I see a ship hit by a bomb. Some of the aircrew in the Blenheim anti-shipping force were promoted to the status of Squadron Commander within a year, having previously held the rank of Sergeant Pilot. The only requirement was to survive.

On one occasion we collected the remnants of a Blenheim flight and kept a safe eye on them as they set course for East Anglia and I instinctively scanned the area in the region of the convoy which was now behind us. I spotted what looked to be the white, creaming wake left by a fast cruising E boat; then I realized that even an E boat could not proceed at such speed. I told the senior section leader to maintain escort on the Blenheims and with my number two turned towards the Dutch coast in order to investigate. There materialized a Blenheim with one engine issuing clouds of white smoke, flying very low over the sea which had caused me to imagine it to be an E boat. We closed on him in formation one on each wing, and I saw the Captain grin with relief. He then switched off his damaged engine, feathered the prop. and gained height very very slowly until he arrived at an altitude of about one thousand feet. We stayed in close escort with him flying virtually at the stall and in this manner we all arrived over the East Anglian coast. We waved good-bye when I indicated by waggling my wings that we had to leave as we were now getting short of fuel and, in any case, could have given him no further assistance.

I learned later that this Blenheim crashed on landing killing the crew.

Later in the year another curious plan was thought up, which was to dispatch a force of about fifty Blenheims flying at ground level with the intention of bombing a power station not far from Essen – in daylight. Our task once again was to deploy to an airfield in Suffolk, pick up the force at Antwerp on its return from the target and escort it home. For this purpose we were given the services of a Blenheim which we would follow as it navigated us over the sea to Antwerp. Through a re-organization in Fighter Command there were by now wing leaders established in the rank of Wing Commander. Our wing leader was, unfortunately, short of combat experience as he had previously been confined to flying instructor duties, and I expect it was for this reason that he made a grave error of judgement. He was leading the wing close behind our navigational Blenheim which was spearheading our operation, but as we approached the Belgian coast, he failed to maintain close enough contact. He was leading three squadrons of Spitfires and he allowed the Wing to fall a mile behind the Blenheim, the pilot of which did not necessarily know anything about this unfortunate lapse, and who consequently crossed the Belgian coast heading towards Antwerp according to his brief and with the greatest gallantry.

Then I saw a spot materialize in the form of a Me 109

diving in a head-on attack directed at the Blenheim. We were much too far behind to give any assistance, and it turned out to be about the finest example of marksmanship I ever witnessed. The 109 dived head-on at the Blenheim, I saw smoke issuing from his gun ports, and the Blenheim immediately exploded in mid-air. Apart from the fate of the aircrew in the Blenheim, this was sheer insolence, considering that not far behind his target were thirty-six Spitfires, and I saw red. The 109 passed under the wing of the Spitfires, naturally enough, as it was on a head-on course. I instinctively broke formation to starboard and said not a word to James, which was a breach of the rule against leaving the formation without the Squadron Commander's authority – unless involved in a mêlée. But I had only one thought in my mind; to kill that skilful German pilot.

He was flying at full throttle and turned immediately for the Belgian coast; I naturally opened up to *Buster* in chase. But the Spitfire had only about ten mph speed advantage over the Me 109 in those days, and although I chased him for some twenty miles into Belgian territory there seemed to be little prospect that I could ever catch up with him before my fuel ran out. I turned for home, throttled back to high boost, and flew at treetop level over the flat Belgian landscape to avoid being hit by flak, crossed the coast and continued over the sea. Instinctively I glanced in my rear-view mirror and there he was about fifteen hundred yards behind me. He was obviously flying at *Buster* so I gave LZ–X emergency boost once again, but this would take a little time to materialize in terms of acceleration. I was now in a tight position; the tables, so to speak, were turned. I dropped her down until the prop was almost hitting the waves, thereby making myself a more difficult target; black smoke issued from the exhaust stubs and I was sweating with fright. The German pilot had closed range to about twelve hundred yards but at sea level I would be a difficult target and the recoil of his cannon when he fired on me would immediately reduce his speed by about thirty mph which would be to my advantage.

Then I saw a cloud, just a little cumulus cloud, hanging in the air at about one thousand feet. I hauled back on the stick, made a tight turn around it, maintained the G and came out on his tail. He was probably out of my range, notwithstanding which I gave him a long burst but saw no strikes on his fuselage. But that was enough to send him off to Brussels to join up with his Belgian girlfriend for the night. I throttled right back to conserve fuel as I had used too much on *Buster* tactics, also to nurse the Merlin on a long flight over the sea, and landed in East Anglia without trouble. I felt ashamed, however, as I had broken military discipline by my intuitive action when I spotted this bastard who had destroyed our Blenheim, but James did not remark on this. Nor did the wing leader; the destruction of the Blenheim and the death of its crew was, in any case, his error of judgement.

We all make mistakes now and again, I suppose.

James was promoted in the summer of 1941 and sent off to a staff appointment; this annoyed him although he had been given a long enough innings on operations. Before he left he took me to his favourite five star hotel, gave me a meal and far too much to drink. On the way back to the airfield he managed to wipe the wing off the car, the Squadron Commander's car, which was in fact now mine, as I had been given command of the squadron. I ticked him off very severely for breaking up my car but our Sergeant blacksmith put a new wing on in no time at all and no one would have known the difference.

I expect I was given command of the squadron on James's recommendation. It was a fairly awe-inspiring responsibility for a chap who was still in his twenty-first year. It is all very well to lead the squadron in the air when the boss takes a day off, quite another thing to assume full command over some two hundred airmen, thirty pilots and twenty-four Spitfires together with supporting equipment worth about £1,000,000.

I need not have worried: I had an adjutant who was an old RFC pilot and had been in the City before the war, not that he lasted long as they court-martialled him for pinching petrol from one of the bowsers for his car. Petrol was rationed, of course, for private motorists but we splashed it around like water for the Spitfires. They coloured it green and the Special Investigation Branch used to swoop on our cars now and again, siphon out samples, have it analysed, and thereby gain proof positive that Air Force petrol was being illicitly used. But I was given another adjutant in due course, and I had an Intelligence Officer, Happy Harpic having long departed for some miserable establishment which might have suited his miserly mind rather better. But my new IO was another Oxford don who proved to be a fount of advice with no axe to grind, and he and I became firm friends. It was against his advice when I made the first of my most grievous errors of judgement, which was indicative of my immaturity. Julian Parker, the IO in question, came into my office one day and suggested that Pickles deserved the DFC.

Of course Pickles deserved the DFC, if not the DFC and bar. He'd sunk in his Spitfire to a depth of twenty-five fathoms, he had knocked down forty large trees in a Spitfire and got away with it, he was filled with vibrant energy, showed the utmost courage on operations, was keen, alert – if over-stretched. But the norm in those days was that you had to be credited with six German aircraft destroyed before you were preferred for the award of the decoration. As with most things the Air Staff laid their hands on, this was a crazy policy, and I had no doubt that I could have broken the system and got Pickles a DFC because I knew how to write a good citation; furthermore the Sector Commander who would have to forward the citation was a chum of mine. But Pickles's record showed that despite his general enthusiasm he was cited only with a score of two and a half German aircraft confirmed as destroyed. Nevertheless, I lost a couple of nights' sleep brooding over Julian's suggestion because it was a fundamental decision – why have awards for gallantry in the face of the enemy if you don't recommend such awards? Having wrestled with the decision, I told Julian that I felt I should not write the citation, although I knew in my bones that Pickles deserved the medal. If I put it forward on his account, however, I might be denigrating the medal so to speak, and I felt that would be wrong in principle.

Julian nodded his head gravely and acquiesced. He knew it was a difficult decision for me to make and also that I had thought long and hard about it. Pickles was posted to an Operational Conversion Unit shortly afterwards, one of his pupils collided with him and cut off the tail off his Spitfire. Pickles fell to his death – without a DFC sewn on to his tunic. I could have murdered myself when I received the news.

The procedures for the award of decorations in the RAF were muddled, in the early years of the war at least. Only one Victoria Cross, to my knowledge, was awarded to a Fighter Pilot in 1940 and he gained this honour on his first ever operational sortie. As previously related, Jasper was given no decoration for gallantry although, in my view, he deserved a DSO if not a bar to a DSO. Another Squadron Commander was awarded the DSO for his squadron's exploits, yet he claimed not one German aircraft destroyed on his own account. In Pickles's case, I should have used my common sense and to hell with the stupid regulations which demanded that six confirmed kills should be the minimum for the award of the Distinguished Flying Cross. Things

101

soon changed as the war wore on, and in comparison decorations flowed more or less like water. Small consolation to his memory, perhaps, but I consider that I was as hard done by as Pickles in similar terms.

This is not blowing my own trumpet as, in any case, the horn has worn away, merely an attempt to give an illustration of the theme. When I, for example, fought back against a Messerschmitt pilot with my right, my master arm, hanging limply down. I was in great pain from a severe flesh wound and seriously bruised knuckles on that hand. It was quite a performance for me to pilot my Spitfire with my left hand well enough to get it down and land, let alone continue in a dogfight with a murderous German pilot who held all the tactical advantages – and more. Yet, I managed to get on to his tail and within 250 yards of him, and to place him easily in my gunsight. If my guns had worked, it is not impossible to say that someone or other might have considered putting me up for the Victoria Cross. Yet I made all the movements necessary to gain a VC, but then my guns would not fire, so where do these things begin and end? If I had rammed him, which was my intention at one moment, no one would have known anything about the action although, presumably, it would have been worthy of a VC if anyone had known the circumstances.

On another occasion, when I was in Cornwall with a make-learn Sergeant Pilot as my number two, we were vectored on to a raid sixty miles south of Start Point, well out over the relentless Atlantic. We engaged three Heinkel bombers covered by six Messerschmitt 109s. Engine failure alone would have brought about death from exposure within ten minutes of being in the sea, to say nothing of the risks of battle damage when taking on a force which outnumbered us by over four to one. However, I destroyed two German aircraft and probably destroyed another and we both got back to base unscathed. A little later in the war, any such action would have meant the immediate award of the DSO. Yet all I got for my troubles was a Distinguished Flying Cross for having a confirmed total of six German aircraft destroyed. In fact, to my certain knowledge, I destroyed ten and probably destroyed or damaged a further ten. I was wounded three times in action, crash-landed three or four times, and baled out once. If any of my readers thinks this is a 'line shoot' he is wrong. It is merely a true summary of events and of the award granted to me in consequence – because the system had not been properly organized at that time in the war. In any case, what the hell does it matter? It is really quite unimportant to me.

But when Pickles was posted I was the only surviving pilot of the summer of 1940 left with the squadron. I have no idea how many pilots came and went, how many became casualties and so on. My guess is that at least a hundred pilots must have been members of the squadron in the year and more I had been with it. The fact that it must have been rather rare for an acting Pilot Officer to arrive at his squadron and assume command not much over a year later never occurred to me at the time. The squadron was my life and there seemed an inexorable logic to it all. One benefit I received was that some of the long service ground personnel who had been Corporals when I first arrived were now my senior NCOs. I knew them very well and they knew me well enough.

One of the most difficult problems war time Squadron Commanders had involved a condition among pilots known as 'lack of moral fibre'. Flying in war time conditions is a fairly nerve-racking business as might by now be evident. Most chaps took such strain well enough; and the strains were not merely confined to combat conditions but also included the sheer dangers in flying what were fairly primitive aircraft by today's standards, together with almost non-existent navigational and landing aids. The weather is an almost inconsequential factor for modern pilots, but to us at that time it was as dangerous a mistress in normal flying as the sun was a fickle master in combat conditions. To be a good pilot requires a high sense of anticipation; to be an effective flying leader demands a deep-probing judgement of other men, combined with a sharp degree of intuition. Taking due note of pilots in combat conditions and testing their responses on the ground, sharpens one's instincts to the extent that one almost knows what a man's thoughts are likely to be before the idea enters his head.

If this appreciation has any merit, it was not surprising that when the adjutant ushered in a newly joined Sergeant Pilot for his formal interview with his future Squadron Commander, I looked at him and the radar in my head began to buzz. From all sorts of strange pieces one very quickly completes the jig-saw puzzle. I was never a martinet, rather to the contrary; my method of getting my way was to employ a somewhat faded charm; but I had certain standards below which no one should descend if they were to stay with my unit. I took one look at this newly joined pilot, and with an almost blinding clarity, I knew that he lacked moral fibre, that he was as yellow as a newborn chick. This assessment was due entirely to instinct. So I then set out to confirm the inner knowledge I already possessed. A silly little thing maybe, but he was wearing brown kid gloves and one does not normally arrive for one's first formal interview improperly dressed. Next, his cap was set on one side of his head rather as Admiral Beatty used to wear his naval cap. Then, his salute was as sloppy as they came, his buttons were badly polished and he wore an over-confident smirk on his face. I invited him to sit down which he did, crossed his legs as if he were lounging at home with dear old Mum, and I inspected his Pilot's logbook, simultaneously keeping up a

Fighter Squadron, 1950. Myself centre front

Ab initio pilot in Tiger Moth, the type
of aircraft in which I made my first flight

Squadron aerobatic team off to Cannes

The 'Fighting Cocks' in cross-formation

Squadron spree. Squadron Commander reclining

Myself in 1952 when in command of the 'Fighting Cocks'

The day I soloed the Javelin

Myself in Churchillian mood

running barrage of questions. The jigsaw was then complete.

I ticked him off for being improperly dressed, warned him that he wouldn't last long on my squadron unless he met the standards, told him he had been appointed to 'A' Flight under Flight Lieutenant Hulton's command, informed him that he would be placed on an immediate disciplinary charge if, for example, he wore kid gloves again when in uniform, and told him to get the hell out.

I thereupon rang up George Hulton.

'Dis is de Boss, Georgie boy,' I said. (I tended to perpetuate the East Side jargon invented by Jasper. Why not maintain a squadron tradition?)

'Yeah boss, yeah,' George replied.

Then I got down to brass tacks and told George that I wanted him to keep a very careful eye on the newly joined Sergeant Pilot, that he should fly with him whenever possible, that he should not allow him to fly his first operational sortie without my consent and that, in any case, I wanted personally to lead him on his first operational flight. I did not explain my inner motivation to George. Three weeks later, however, George came into my office, saluted and sprawled his bulky frame on the creaking wicker chair which comprised the greater part of my office furniture; the lesser part of the furniture, another but smaller wicker chair was occupied by my dog. George pulled from his tunic pocket a battered old pipe, lit it and then gazed at me with a grave face.

'Sir,' he said. 'In my view, Sergeant Pilot Hogg is lacking in moral fibre. I think he should be suspended from flying duties and reported to the medicos.'

'Why do you feel like that, George?' I inquired, acting innocent as a virgin.

'Instinct, partly. On the other hand, he has tried to land his aircraft twice under my nose with his undercart still retracted. Further to that, I don't like his attitudes which are to put it mildly, brash – leaning towards insolence. In fact, I believe that he is intent on getting himself kicked off the squadron for personal reasons based on lack of nerve.'

'Thanks for your opinion,' I told George. 'Would you fix a convoy patrol some time this afternoon and I will fly with Hogg on his first operational sortie. That is to say if you believe that flying a convoy patrol is really operation as opposed to being a bloody boring routine patrol.'

'Sure will,' George replied. 'I'll give you a half hour's warning, and I'll detail Hogg as your number two.'

George saluted, put his pipe back in his mouth, and left. I brooded over the situation.

The jig-saw was now complete. Hogg was a verbose little cockney who assumed an air of over-confidence when, in fact, he was introverted out of his wits. The only reason he applied to be a pilot in the RAF was to be awarded the flying brevet, or wings, then he would be in a better position to impress his girlfriends in his local pub. Having got his wings, he might, he assumed, with luck, be posted to a target towing flight, a non-operational unit, when he could then continue to wear his wings and thus keep up the pressure on his girlfriends to maintain their legs in a wide-apart position. Where he was sadly disappointed was when he received a signal posting him to a fighter squadron. So, he had turned up for his first interivew with me improperly dressed, he tried to needle me into kicking him out without further ado, but without success. Then he attempted to impress George that his pilot ability was not up to standard by using the usual method of those who are lacking in moral fibre, which was to belly-land your aircraft and pretend that you had forgotten to put the undercart down. It was not a particularly dangerous manoeuvre to belly-land a Spitfire in cold blood; but it did cost the country many hundreds of pounds to have that aircraft repaired.

George rang up in the afternoon and told me that I was detailed to take off with Sergeant Pilot Hogg at four pm to relieve Green section over a convoy which would be about thirty miles from Falmouth when we arrived, but he would give me up-dated intelligence on this when I was ready to take to the air. I drove to his flight office where I kept my flying kit, got togged up and told Hogg that he was to stay on my wing until he received further instructions in the air. We took off, and he flew quite well in formation, passed over somewhere like Land's End and intercepted the convoy. I kept out of range of their pom-poms because the Navy were particularly trigger happy, called up Green Leader and told him I was in position, so he could now return to base.

'Yeah boss, yeah,' he said over the R/T, and vanished from my sight with his number two.

I sidled stealthily within range of the convoy in case the Navy thought we were a couple of Me 109s, told Hogg to stay about 400 yards behind me for the time being, and that I would be making continual orbits of the convoy. We kept this up for about half an hour, then I called him up on the R/T, told him to come up in close formation, saw him nicely settled in on my wingtip and then cried wolf.

'Red two,' I screamed over the R/T. 'I see six bandits, range two miles, nine o'clock high. Line astern *Go!*' Just to rub it in, I then said, 'I recognize them as Messerschmitts. Put your gun button to *Fire*. Prepare for extreme evasive manoeuvres!'

I never saw Hogg again until I met him in my office. He did a bunk. I continued to circle the convoy alone until the next section detailed for the chore told me they were in sight of it, whereupon I returned to base. I interviewed Hogg when I landed – he was still in his flying clothing – and asked him why he had deserted in the face of the 'enemy'. He made the usual excuses none of which was valid. His glycol temperature started reading high and then a red warning light came on. What red warning light I asked because there was no warning light tied into the coolant system. He became confused, so, just to make confusion worse confounded, I inquired why he had not rung me up on the R/T to inform me he was returning to base. There was only one possible lie in reply to this and he used it. His R/T plug must have slipped out of the socket he said, but this was virtually impossible.

I dismissed him and wrote out a report affirming that in my view this pilot suffered from lack of moral fibre, that fear was dominant in his mind to the exclusion of all rational thinking, showed it to George who agreed with it, and gave it to Hogg to read and countersign. Then I told him to get the hell out, and report immediately to the RAF Depot at Uxbridge to await further proceedings. I did not want that rat contaminating the air around my squadron any longer. The form was stamped Medical Confidential and finished up with the psychiatrists, many of whom were women doctors who did not know the arse-end of an aircraft from the front. It took them nine months hard work to confirm what I knew in my bones to be true in thirty seconds flat.

In due course they removed Hogg's flying brevet, reduced him in rank to aircraftsman and posted him to the RAF Regiment. I hope he got shot. If so, it would indubitably have been in the back.

Another aspect of psychiatry we came up against was the business of selecting pilots for various roles. Again many of the doctors were women, and in my view hopelessly unfitted for such a nice judgement. I could tell a potentially superb fighter pilot just by talking to him let alone flying with him on my wing. One such was a Sergeant Pilot called Bob Small. He was the right size for a fighter pilot – small; he twitched like an aspen leaf, lived right on the end of his nerves, had cat-like reflexes and bit his nails. He was raring to go but had little opportunities with a squadron stuck down in Cornwall, and he kept coming into my office pleading to be sent where the action was hotter, and although he was a nice guy he began to bore me with his impatience. Then I received a signal requiring me to detail a pilot to an Eleven Group squadron where they were making fighter sweeps over France and running into a lot of trouble with FW 190s, especially as at this time – natural marksmen and experienced pilots apart – the average British fighter pilot did not know how to shoot straight. So I rang up Bob Small and told him to come and see me. He entered my office with a hopeful look in his eye.

'Bob,' I said, 'I've got some bad news for you.'

Hope faded from his face.

'I've had to institute the duty for squadron NCO pilots to take their turn in the chore as Orderly Sergeant. I'm afraid you'll have to do a twenty-four hour stint commencing at 0630 hours tomorrow. Which means, of course, that you cannot fly for that period, you will have to wear your best uniform, attend the flag raising ceremony and so on. In short, you will have a large administrative load on your lap.'

'What me! No flying! Administration! – Nobody told me anything about administration when I became a pilot!'

His face reflected utter despair so I let him off the hook.

'I'm pulling your leg, Bob,' I said. 'As a matter of fact you're posted to Eleven Group. Pack your bags and get on the train.'

It took him five seconds, open-mouthed, to suck in this gem of information. Then his face lit up, he chuckled with joy, rushed up to me, shook me warmly by the hand and then literally did three cartwheels en route to the door which he struck with a resounding thump and fell back, a glazed expression on his face.

'Aren't you sorry to be leaving the squadron, you ungrateful bum?' I asked severely.

'Sorry, sir,' he said, 'I just want to get where the action's hottest.'

I never knew what happiness was until I witnessed this performance by Bob Small. He went on to get the DFM, a commission and a DFC and bar – and he survived the war.

Even women psychiatrists could have placed Bob as a fighter pilot, and the basis of their judgement would have been the negative approach. It was obvious that he did not possess the incredible fortitude needed to be a successful bomber pilot, that he would be no good sitting on his backside for eight hours, relentlessly maintaining course for Berlin and hopefully back again, while the biggest firework display the world ever saw was issuing from German soil aimed in his general direction. They would never have recommended him for flying instructor duties as he lacked responsibility, no matter the fact that he was an exceptional and natural pilot. Coastal Command duties were also out for Bob as was the rest of the gamut aerial operations in the war. If he had been told to fly a Catalina flying-boat for a 17 hour sortie gazing at the inhospitable Atlantic Ocean or the even more inhospitable Pacific Ocean, he would have vomited with sheer, unadulterated boredom. Fighter pilots can only keep up the tempo in short bursts; then they need to sleep. I can go to sleep at any time of the day, merely for ten minutes, at the drop of a hat. We called it cat-napping.

But these bloody psychiatrists should have adopted a positive policy in the case of Paul Wimsey, as I noted the moment he entered my office for his formal interview on joining the squadron. He was one of the nicest men I ever met, tall, ruddy of complexion, slow and deliberate, with charming manners – and he smoked a pipe. His nails were immaculately trimmed because he did not bite them. I chatted to him about this and that, saw that he had been given an average assessment as a trainee pilot, that he had done sufficient flying to be posted to an operational squadron, and immediately assessed him as the perfect chap for Coastal Command duties and next in priority Bomber Command. However, I could hardly tell him that as he must be given the chance to prove my judgement wrong. So I appointed him to George's flight, told George to give him a lot of flying in the shortest possible time and let me have a report within a month. George's report confirmed my suspicions, so I had Paul in, sat him down and talked to him like a father although he was about four years older than I was.

I came in with the indirect approach, hinting that he might be better employed elsewhere, underlining the fact that we enjoyed his company very much, that he was a considerable asset to the squadron – which was true – but I was a little concerned with his speed of reflexes and so on. Paul was by no means affronted, merely disappointed in my general assessment as to his potential as a fighter pilot. He counter-argued seriously with me, blue smoke issuing from his pipe. I put the proposition that it was fine and dandy to be with us while we were, so to speak, on rest. But sooner or later the squadron would be redeployed to a hotter operational climate and might he not get bullets up his bum? He eventually saw my point of view, confessed that he by no means felt in the marrow of his bones that he would ever make a brilliant fighter pilot. Notwithstanding, might he not be allowed to stay with the squadron?

He had found his métier with this squadron, he explained, he loved the life, he got on very well with the chaps; why he even loved me! I relented – I had no other recourse, told him that we very much enjoyed having him with us, slapped him on the back, pointed out that in his case his first priority *must* be self-protection and I didn't give a damn if he never shot down a German aircraft, wished him good luck, told

111

him that he would be included on the normal operational roster as that was his wish, and he departed a happy man.

Then the rock apes who tended to inhabit the Air Ministry at this time thought it would be a good idea to send in a large formation of bombers, by daylight, to attack *Scharnhorst* and *Gneisenau* which had slipped into the anchorage at Brest. They had been attempting to destroy these capital ships by night attacks with no success whatsoever. My squadron, plus the other few 'long range' fighter units, were the only forces available to escort these bombers on the long and hazardous flight across the turbulent Atlantic to Brest, so we intercepted the bomber force when it was en route to Brest and deployed ourselves round them as best we could in the light of the paucity of our resources. What the rock apes might have failed to appreciate was that Brest was the most heavily defended target in the world at that time in terms of flak, nor was it short of fighter defences.

So these admirable aircrews, flying in the bombers, proved to me once again their sheer fortitude as they penetrated to the target area and all bloody hell came up from the ground. Never in my life have I seen so many bombers blazing in mid-air, never have I seen so many parachutes drifting through the fair skies of France with men under their canopies. It was no part of our job to penetrate the flak barrage, merely to attempt to keep German fighters at bay and, in any case, they would not attack the bombers while they were in the middle of the barrage. What was left of the bomber force made an ungainly wheel when they got away from the flak and we picked them up on the other side of the barrage. A bunch of Me 109s came in and we countered the attack while the other escorting British fighter squadrons saw the bombers safely back over the Atlantic and out of range of the German fighter defences. I got in only one short burst of fire and I doubt whether any squadron pilot claimed a kill, but we fended them off notwithstanding.

When we landed back I had a roll-call. One of our pilots was missing. His name was Paul Wimsey. I could have cut my hand off. I should have been more persuasive.

SEVEN

NON-OPERATIONAL

THE ideologists on the staff of HQFC decided, in 1941, to lay down a norm for operational flying. Bomber Command had adopted a system whereby members of aircrew who had performed thirty raids over Germany should be posted on non-operational duties to allow their quivering nerve-ends to recover. In Fighter Command, it was then thought, two hundred flying hours on serious operations should similarly demand a pilot's posting to non-operational duties. Even the staff had the sense to appreciate, however, that convoy patrols were only quasi-operational, so they calculated that one hour flown over convoys should rank only as a half-hour's operation in terms of the two hundred hours maximum. At the time the edict came down from the high altar, I had flown about four hundred hours on real operations and a couple of hundred over convoys so I was vulnerable in terms of being chucked off the squadron for a rest from operations, and as I had no intention of allowing this to happen, I began to fiddle the books. My system worked, and at any time I could *prove* that I had flown only one hundred and fifty operational hours and there the figure stuck. But they caught me out in 1942 and I was almost forcibly removed from my command and sent off to run a non-operational squadron.

Two things happened when I took up this new command.

First I suffered from acute insomnia and hardly slept for three weeks as the strain of not being under operational orders bit. The stresses of being operational were, of course on a considerably greater scale but one had got used to this extraordinary way of life, where one saw the dawn rise almost every day and lived in a state of constant tension awaiting the order to scramble. To put it another way, one's metabolism was completely awry. On the other hand, my new squadron had no less than six different types of aircraft on the inventory, which gave me an opportunity to enjoy the thrill of flying new types. At this stage I had flown only Tiger Moths, Hart Variants, Harvards, Magisters and Spitfires, but I now had in my hands Hurricanes, Ansons, Oxfords, Blenheims, Proctors and Lockheed Hudsons. The Hurricane, I considered, was a complete cab horse compared to the Spitfire, but I greatly enjoyed flying the American Hudson which was the first big aircraft I ever piloted, and it could carry by the standards of the day a large posse of passengers. I knew nothing of navigation, of course, apart from following railway lines and such like features, but on the other hand the Hudson had an endurance of several hours so even I had plenty of time to find my way home before I ran out of fuel.

The Americans prefer to fight their wars with plenty of perquisites, such as one-armed bandits, chewing-gum, blonde ladies laid on without having to make the effort to go out and find them and so on. Possibly because the British do not possess an infinite defence budget for such purposes, more likely because they tend to consider a military chap, whether in the Navy, Army or Air Force, as a kind of puritanical soldier of Cromwell who believes in slaying in the name of the Lord and all that sort of nonsense, they tend to design their military hardware in what the Americans would describe as a hard-arsed format. Every British military aircraft I have flown has been actually uncomfortable; every

American military aircraft I have flown has been, by comparison, the lap of luxury. There is sense in both points of view, but whereas the British leaned too far in one direction, it might be true to say that the Americans leaned just a little too far the other way.

I very much enjoyed flying the Hudson although I flew it very badly and could never land it without bouncing. What I did not appreciate at this stage was that the Hudson was a very dangerous aircraft to bounce on landing because, if one hit the ground hard enough, an oleo leg could easily penetrate the fuel tanks and one would finish up in a blazing wreck with not the slightest prospect of getting out in time. But the pilot's seat in the Hudson was a veritable armchair, and they provided a piddle tube which allowed one to urinate when in flight. Next, the Americans like lots of knobs, switches and gauges, to say nothing of copious warning lights. I could hardly comprehend any one of these indicators which concerned a hundred different instrument systems, whereas the Spitfire contained only about four. But, apart from gaining some experience of flying new types, I hated every moment of my time with this non-operational squadron and was duly kicked out in short time, much to my gratification.

I had greased the wheel of the machine, which would inevitably have ejected me in any case, by volunteering to go as air adviser to the First Airborne Division in the British Army, which had not long been formed. This was quite out of my line of country but I doubt whether I have ever enjoyed myself so much since. On the one hand, the Army made me giggle; on the other a nicer bunch of chaps it would hardly have been possible to meet. They were terribly serious about their paper work, for example, whereas in the squadrons we tended to put it on the fire if it were too difficult to comprehend. Possibly this was because our paper work was usually a pathetic jumble of nonsense, whereas

116

theirs might have contained something of importance. The commander of the division was Major General 'Boy' Browning, famous for being the best-dressed officer in the British Army, one-time officer in the Grenadier Guards, and he would most certainly have died with his boots clean. In the Division there were County regiments, Guards regiments and Light Infantry regiments. I loved the manner in which they moved at different paces on the march when on parade. The Guards were long-legged and slow, the Light Infantry practically jog-trotted. If I had had to perform a forced march in a light infantry regiment, I would have had a heart attack in about five minutes flat.

General Browning liked to have an airman around because he did, after all, command the First Airborne Division. Part of my job was gently to introduce his soldiers to the ways of the air, but he could probably have made a better choice than me for that. I used to give lectures to the soldiers in an attempt to explain some of the intricacies of the air, and he used to take me with him when he performed some of his inspections. That he was unconventional can be indicated by the fact, or so I believe it to be, that when he was the adjutant at Sandhurst, leading the passing-out parade towards the main building, long before the war, he all of a sudden decided to ride his charger up the steps of the Royal Military Academy behind the parade. This is now a most important tradition at Sandhurst and his successors carry it out to this day. What his Commandant said to him when he originally committed this offence I will never know.

But my office was in the headquarters of the Air Landing Brigade which was equipped with gliders. The brigade was commanded by Brigadier 'Hoppy' Hopkins who was a most remarkable man, a scholar, a civil pilot and with about six times the courage I possessed. I used gently and regularly to pull his leg, so he decided to pull mine. As I was now part of the Army, so to speak, I tended to wear RAF battledress in the same way as they wore battledress, with their insignia, which was the Pegasus, sewn on to the shoulders as that was the manner in which they preferred to wear the badge. Then I also wore a maroon coloured beret as that was part of their headgear, and my Army batman removed my RAF badge from one of my old caps and sewed it on to the beret.

This, of course, was right outside RAF dress procedures and Hoppy knew it although he liked it. So he bided his time and then suggested that I should accompany him on a visit to his old outfit which had its headquarters in London and was the Phantom reconnaissance unit. There we met such nice people as David Niven, film actor, one-time regular soldier, back again in the army for the duration. I knew that Hoppy was planning something when he suggested that we had supper in his club before returning to Newbury where the brigade headquarters was based, because it showed in the twinkle in his eye. His club was the United Services, popularly known as the Senior, and I followed him in wearing RAF battledress with Pegasuses sewn on both shoulders, a maroon beret with a RAF cap badge and other accoutrements.

'I think we had better have a very quick buffet supper,' Hoppy suddenly said to me.

'Sure, sir,' I replied. 'But what's the hurry?'

'I've just seen at least three Air Marshals rushing up to the library.'

'So what?'

'I have a nasty feeling they are about to read up RAF dress regulations.'

So we got the hell out.

When my 'rest' from operations was coming to an end, I pulled some strings and was given command of another Spitfire squadron, as the existing Squadron Commander had been promoted to Wing Commander on seniority. Thus he was, so to speak, kicked upstairs. He, however, was an even

118

better string-puller than myself and pleaded to be left in command, although he out-ranked the appointment which was established as Squadron Leader. On my arrival to take over the outfit, I was horrified to learn that I would be held on the squadron as a supernumerary Squadron Leader and that he, the Wing Commander, would retain his command. I checked him out and discovered that he then possessed a quarter of my operational experience, but that I would have to fly on operations under his command. This was a crazy situation because, in my view, he was far less effective in the lead than I was. The rock apes should have appreciated this, of course, and sent me to command another squadron, but in the war, staff work in the RAF was even worse than in peace time.

I stuck it out as long as I could and had the privilege of flying on five sorties during the ill-fated raid on Dieppe in August 1942. There were masses of German fighters in the sky, including the excellent FW 190, and I remember seeing at least five parachutes descending at one time. But these boys in 1942 did it all differently from the way we did in 1940, and although the Spitfire Mark V was faster and more manoeuvrable than the Mark II, although the armament consisted of two 20 mm cannon plus four ·303 inch Browning machine-guns, I reckon that my old squadron with its inadequate armament would have done a lot better over Dieppe on one sortie than the one I was then attached to achieved in five.

I claimed only one Heinkel 111 destroyed and the Intelligence Officer, whom I did not know, checked it out and confirmed it. Later, he informed me that he had changed his mind and given it to another claimant. This was nonsense and spurious as well, but I didn't argue. The whole thing stank in my nostrils so I was glad when they sent me off to do a course on fighter gunnery. This came about because, on diagnosing the ciné camera films exposed over Dieppe,

where there were hundreds of fighter combats and in consequence yards of film, the scientific analysts compared them
with the pilots' combat reports and came to the startling
conclusion that three quarters of the pilots in Fighter Command could not shoot straight. A top priority programme
was immediately put into action whereby a new gunsight
was developed based on gyros and servo-mechanisms; but
they needed experienced, senior fighter pilots to undergo
courses to evaluate this gunsight, use it against high speed
drogues and return to the sector stations to teach squadron
pilots these new arts.

I hated the chore but it had its advantages. In the complex
of airfields which comprised my sector, there were squadrons equipped with various fighter types. If I was supposed
to be a gunnery training officer then, in my view, I should be
allowed to keep myself in practice by flying operational
sorties. So I flew on fighter sweeps in Spitfires Marks XII
and IV and also in Typhoons. The Typhoon was a large
fighter fitted with a Napier Sabre engine which was unre-
liable, but it carried a heavy weight of armament and later
rockets, was very fast, and useful in attacks on coastal ship-
ping. But all in all I was again just part of the sediment, back
to square one, despite my considerable experience of fighter
operations, and my high score of enemy kills. My personal
disposition, in any case, was inhibited by the fact that a
famous buccaneer, Captain Sir Henry Morgan, was my an-
cestor, and like him, I tended strenuously to object to being
buggered about by bureaucrats. He, incidentally, was carted
back to England from the Spanish Main under close arrest
for some imagined misdemeanour. Whereupon, Charles II
dubbed him knight and returned him to Jamaica as lieuten-
ant-governor. He died later of alcoholic poisoning, but I'm
all right because I hate the taste of Jamaica rum.

My job had even more perquisites than those already described. I could never get the squadron pilots into the lecture

hall to see their ciné-films, where I could explain how they went wrong, without some sort of bait. Accordingly, I found a source which provided me with blue films, ciné-bleu, and I would tempt them with one to start the proceedings and promise them another at the end. In the middle, they had to watch their own films which might indicate that they were out of range, short of deflection, or lead, when opening fire against a crossing target, or that they had not appreciated sufficiently well the flight attitude of the target. Fixed gun fighter marksmanship is a highly complex business and these chaps were not Cambridge Wranglers. The arts of fighter aiming rely to an inordinate extent on mathematics, but I think they improved as time went on. I never had much trouble with sighting my guns because I was a keen pheasant shot and curiously, the arts of killing a pheasant on the wing are similar to those required when shooting down a member of the Luftwaffe.

Another of my tasks was to introduce the Americans to Fighter Command interception methods, and the particular unit I was involved with was equipped with Thunderbolts, a great big heavy fighter with an enormous radial engine. I met up with the American major commanding the Thunderbolt unit who was a nice guy, and we planned a programme of lectures for his pilots – even his ground crews because a fighter scramble depends on absolute co-operation between mechanics and pilots. But if I was detailed to assist the USAAF, I reckoned that they could also do me a favour, so I asked the Major a question.

'I can't give you proper assistance in learning British interception methods,' I told him, 'unless I have an appreciation of the Thunderbolt. So what about authorizing me to fly in one?'

'Sure, sure,' he said, having taken the cigar out of his mouth. 'Just go and tell the chief technician to get one of the birds ready for you.'

I love the casual American approach although it might have changed somewhat by now. I sauntered up to the chief technician and asked him if he would get one of the birds ready for me to fly.

'Sure,' he replied, having removed the cigar from his mouth. 'I'll have one on the line in a half hour.'

I climbed aboard to find a maze of switches, gauges, knobs and a urinating tube. He gave me the thumbs up signal and I beckoned him on to the wing. He climbed aboard with a puzzled expression on his face.

'Is there any trouble, sir?' he inquired.

'Not really, chief. But how do you start up this bird?'

'Oh, that's simple enough.'

The thumping great radial engine moved the enormous propeller around in a haze of white smoke, I waved the chocks away and then realized I didn't even know the stalling speed of the bird, nor the approach speed for landing, nor for that matter what any of the instruments indicated, apart from the flying panel. However, I taxied it to the up-wind end of the runway, lined her up and pushed the throttle open to its full extent. Very little seemed to happen. Sure, she rolled up the runway, and indeed she rolled rather faster as time went on. She seemed to be producing full boost according to the gauge, but she evidently was not getting anywhere near to take-off speed. By now I was running out of options, as we were half-way up the runway, and even if I had throttled back and stuffed the brakes on to their full extent, they would have burned out and I would have finished up in the main street of the local town unless I hit a tree en route. So there was nothing to do except to sweat it out and pray.

At about the last possible moment, I hauled back on the stick and the bird leapt into the air like a hen full of eggs. I kept her low until she built up speed and then put her into the climb. From this point she transformed herself from a pinioned swan to a wild goose. Her rate of climb was poor but she was as light as a feather on the controls. I climbed her up to thirty thousand feet and then half-rolled and hauled back into a vertical climb. She went down at the same speed as the Great Pyramid of Gizeh would have done had it been possible to first haul it up to thirty thousand feet before dropping it in an earthwards direction. I hastily hauled her out before she made the first sonic boom in the history of aviation and then played with her. She was incredibly good, her aileron control was out of this world. To roll her was analogous to a catherine wheel spinning round on Guy Fawkes night. For such a large heavy fighter she was perfection but she would never have made a good interceptor because of her slow acceleration; she proved to be an excellent escort fighter, however.

I dived to treetop level and beat up the American dispersal at about four hundred mph, hauled her up and did three vertical rolls and she flicked so swiftly she nearly caused me to black out in the lateral plane. Then I decided to land; then I realized that I had no idea of her approach and landing speeds. But she was fat, she was big, and she was a very heavy aircraft, so I opted for an approach speed of 170 mph – which would be safe enough against a stall on the approach, probably much too fast in fact, I put her down on the runway on to her main wheels at 130 mph and hoped that the brakes were going to stand the strain. They did. I taxied her into the American dispersal and the chief technician came out of his shack, cigar in his mouth, jockey-cap on the back of his head.

'Say, sir,' he said, 'that was a mighty fine landing for your first time up.'

'Thanks, chief,' I replied.

Little did he know I was sweating like a pig with fright.

I became fascinated, hypnotized, by the job of commander

of fighter squadrons. I was a Walter Mitty and they represented my dream world. It needed a bit of luck, a little persuasion and a great deal of machination to ensure that the authorities kept offering one such commands. Now and again I had no option and had to assume other appointments, and my purpose then became to get out of these as soon as possible when I took note that another vacancy as a Squadron Commander was looming on the horizon.

But they caught me out again when they posted me to the appointment as Gunnery/Tactics Staff Officer at Twelve Group Headquarters. My job was to spread the gospel, in terms of tactics and how to shoot straight, to all the fighter squadrons deployed between Alnwick, Chester and Cambridge. But, at this time, Fighter Command was running out of steam as Operation Overlord had been mounted, the Allied armies were in France, and tactical not purely fighter operations were necessary. We were, in short, a bloody great white elephant. If anyone wants to know the derivation of the expression, it came about when the King of Siam presented his neighbour with one of these rare species. He did so because he was indulging in a feud with his neighbour and assumed that the costs of maintaining such a rare animal would eventually bankrupt his enemy. He was plumb right and marched his troops in to capture this adjacent territory without difficulty, because his neighbour hadn't got enough money left to maintain a standing army of sufficient strength to do battle. I forget what happened to the original white elephant.

But my stint of duty at Twelve Group Headquarters was most enjoyable. I had exchanged my Lagonda for a three litre Bentley and I was given extra petrol coupons for the purpose of making staff visits to the stations when the weather was too bad to use the communications aircraft. I drove, time and time again, up a virtually empty Great North Road, and the burble of the Bentley's exhaust was something out of this world. The engine revved at about three thousand maximum which gave the car a speed of over seventy. The noise emanating from the exhaust pipe was, to me, akin to a siren's seductive screech. It was a delicious car, although it took a bit of starting.

Then there were the WAAF officers, mostly girls of high quality possessed of hot fannies. This almost broke my nerve because I was, at this stage, in a condition of holy wedlock. As Oscar Wilde said, the only way to get rid of a temptation is to yield to it. But he, poor old thing, was a rabid homosexual so he might have had more difficulty than I. In any case, fornication normally depends on the male initiative – if it is ever to come off successfully. So I kept these gorgeous young ladies at bay to my own satisfaction, if not to theirs. Then I learned to play bridge, at vast expense. There was a dreadful, smirky, wingless wonder on the Staff, an expert bridge player, who took me on at a shilling a point. He cleaned me out to the tune of ten quid on our first session but I thought I could get the better of him. I was dead wrong. In a fortnight, I lost thirty pounds and decided to retreat and read Culbertson's book on bridge. I would dearly love to meet him again. I reckon he would not leave me today with his pants still covering his duck-like backside, or his shirt.

Although we had virtually nothing to do at Twelve Group Headquarters, my fellow officers were of such high calibre – to say nothing of the WAAF girls – that it was a positively enjoyable experience to be deskbound with only occasional opportunities to fly. We played bridge in our offices, we played poker in the evenings, and we occasionally wrote diatribes to Station Commanders pointing out that they were not aware of their true functions. I sped along the length and breadth of the Midlands and Northern England in the Bentley, and I carried a shotgun and poached pheasants on the way.

But after the Battle of Arnheim in 1944, the Air Officer Commanding had me in and inquired whether I would like to be given another flying appointment.

'Please God, yes,' I replied.

'Please me, yes,' he replied sternly. 'It is within my remit not God's.'

He thereupon gave me command of the senior squadron in the RAF which happened to be under his overall command. Its motto was *In omnibus princeps* which I translated roughly to mean 'there's got to be a first time for everything'. It was equipped with Spitfires Mark XXI but I never had a chance to fly the squadron on real operations before the war ground to a halt.

Some of these Spitfires had five-blade propellers, others had six-bladed propellers, three of each rotating in the contra-prop, disposition. It was the same lovely aircraft as its mother, the Mark I Spitfire. Both the five-bladed and contra-prop Spitfires Mark XXI were dreamy aircraft. The former could exceed the performance of the latter on the dive, but on the climb it was quite a bit slower and could never get as high as the contra-prop. They both retained beautiful handling characteristics. There never was before, and there never will be again, an aircraft of such delicacy as the Spitfire, although today's Trident, I believe, has similar handling qualities and, of course, it can fly at twice the speed of the Spitfire straight and level. (I once flew to Geneva in a Trident, admittedly with the assistance of a tail-wind, at an average ground speed of seven hundred mph.)

There was nothing much to do with my squadron when the war in Europe ended, except to fly on training sorties, drink beer and form a darts team to play against the various darts-clubs based on the villages in the wolds of the East Riding of Yorkshire. It was a snow-ridden winter but, I believe, every winter Yorkshire has ever known led to great downfalls of snow. Such entertainments apart, I found myself with a problem of some magnitude on my hands, involving the general condition of one of my senior pilots.

He had an excellent, if not brilliant, war record, but he had been taken prisoner by the Germans after baling out over occupied Europe, and had spent some time in a POW camp. On his return to England and having been appointed to a fighter squadron, it was clear to me that he had lost his nerve for flying. My predecessor had never ordered him into the air; he had become slack, dissolute even, and spent the working day with much too much beer in his belly. I maintained a watchful brief on him, reviewing his behaviour patterns, and attempted to gain his confidence. The moment arrived when I thought he trusted me so I told him that I wanted him to take a Spitfire off and land it again. He looked startled. If he did not accept this challenge, I said, I would kick him off the squadron; he accepted the challenge, but he needed help.

I assisted him to strap himself into the Spitfire Mark XXI, reminded him about the various knobs and tits, the approach and landing speeds, told him that I would be in the caravan placed at the end of the runway which contained R/T on the local frequency and would give him guidance on his final approach. Then I drove to the caravan at high speed, climbed aboard, and watched him taxiing with some anxiety. His take-off was good enough because, he was, after all, an experienced pilot. I kept in touch with him over the R/T on the local frequency as he played about aloft, relearning the enjoyment of the air, feeling his confidence returning. Then I told him over the R/T that I wanted him to come in on an approach, that he was to overshoot off it and climb away, and I would then give him further instructions.

I criticized his approach for the overshoot in terms of his final turning point – too close to the runway threshold – his flying speed which I adjudged to be too fast, and his simulated point of touch-down which I thought was too far up the runway for safety. He acknowledged my criticisms and his voice was calm. He overshot as instructed and I told him I now wanted him to land the Spitfire, that he should take into account my previous criticisms, that I was going to close down the R/T and he was from this point on his own. He gave a calm reply and I pretended that I had switched off the R/T. In a single-seater fighter there can be only one man in charge – the pilot; no good would come of it if I suddenly bawled at him that he was too high or whatever. My ulcers were quivering by this time as badly, no doubt, as his. I was making an attempt to resuscitate an excellent pilot who had suffered too much travail in the light of the frailty of his human impulses. It was a make or break operation, but I thought it worth the risk.

He came in for his landing high and fast and I grabbed at the microphone with the intention of ordering him to make another overshoot. Then I decided not to. He struck the runway a glancing blow, bounced, maintained control, kept the Spitfire straight up the runway and let the tailwheel drop of its own volition. He was very close to the down-wind threshold of the runway when he stopped, but he didn't make the Spitfire rear on to its nose by braking too hard. He taxied gently back and I was there to meet him. He was a changed man; he had regained his confidence all of a sudden. It was one of the most rewarding experiences in my life.

From that time on, he flew every sortie for which he was detailed. He became, once again, a tower of strength. But, by God, it had put a strain on my nerves.

Meanwhile, I had been electrifying my contacts, men of Air rank who had previously served with the squadron I commanded. It had originally been based on Tangmere, near Chichester: then it was despatched to France in support of the BEF in 1939; it had indeed been based previously on Tangmere since at least 1926. Several of its one-time commanding officers were by now men of considerable influence, and I maintained the pressure that the squadron should be allowed to return to its traditional home now that the war had ended. With great good fortune, the AOC commanding Eleven Group, within whose command Tangmere was, had also been one of its Squadon Commanders and, of course, I made a personal application to him. He took my point, argued the case with the Air Ministry, and lo and behold! I received a signal ordering me to redeploy my squadron from its Yorkshire base to Tangmere. This was a great moment; I wrote the movement order in five minutes flat.

The Advanced Party went on ahead, the Main Party serviced the Spitfires, put them on the line and then set off in convoy to catch, by courtesy of the LNER, a train with special carriages allocated to them. The Rear Party saw 20 Spitfires into the air, and stayed behind to clear up the mess. We scorched southwards at two thousand feet, but as my unfortunate wife was staying with her mother in a house not all that far from Rugby this was one of my pin-points. We passed over her head at a hundred feet with a noise worse than thunder, having opened up to four hundred mph for the purpose. Her cousin's cows which grazed on an adjoining estate gave sour milk for the next fortnight in consequence. The cloud dispersed as we crossed the Thames, ahead lay the Sussex Downs, then we overflew Goodwood racecourse and dived for Tangmere. We came in low and beat up the airfield, pulled up into a slick squadron break and landed one after the other with a couple of seconds between aircraft. When one has the privilege to command a good fighter squadron, a polished landing also becomes a point of honour and it requires a little practice and a lot of criticism before one can be sure the chaps have got the technique absolutely tamed. We, I believe, had it tamed.

Tangmere was indeed pleased to see such a long-established squadron return to its bosom. We were, if anything, even more delighted. It was without question the most pleasant RAF Station in Fighter Command, close to Chichester which is a nice enough town in all conscience, not far from the sea, adjacent to the racecourses at Goodwood and Fontwell, and within the Goodwood estate there is one of the loveliest small eighteen hole golfcourses ever designed. A few of the mess staff had known the squadron in the days of the Hendon Air Pageant, understood its traditions better than I did, and remembered some of the men who made their names when flying with it in ancient biplanes. I had already served at Tangmere on three previous occasions and people like the mess cook, the mess steward and so on were old friends of mine. It was just like coming home.

When we got settled in, the staff at Eleven Group Headquarters decided that units of Fighter Command should perform a fly-past over London to celebrate Victory day. As we had the highest flying aircraft in the Command, our role would be to spearhead the fly-past by flying within the contrail region and laying contrails just before the main formations appeared at low level. The trouble was that no one quite knew where the contrail level lay, nor do they today, except it is a sight easier to form contrails with the excessive heat of a jet engine than by the heat exuded from the exhaust-stubs of a Spitfire. So we made it our job long before the fly-past was due to evaluate contrails, at what mean height did they occur, under what conditions of weather and so on. Day after day we climbed to heights well over forty thousand feet taking note of when the contrails formed; on some occasions they never formed at all. I also took this opportunity to check on the climb ability of the contra-prop Spitfire vis à vis that of the five-bladed propeller type. At about thirty-five thousand feet I would warn my number two flying in a five-blader that I, in the contra-prop, was going to give her full boost and invite him to try to maintain formation on me. He never could; the contra-prop would sail away from him at double his rate of climb. He could always exceed my maximum speed on the dive however.

At dawn on the day of the Victory fly-past I studied the met charts with dismay. There was low cloud at four hundred feet and great layers of thick cloud up to heaven itself. There was not the slightest prospect that the weather would clear in time for the fly-past, so although we might have been able to lay contrails high in the sky, no mortal living in London would ever have seen them. Clearly, the fly-past would have to be cancelled. I waited until nine a.m. when the staff officers staggered into their offices and rang up saying I was proposing to put my Spitfires to bed for the day, but I came up against the senior officer who was so indecisive that he wouldn't have known how to order a willing whore to jump into bed.

'Oh, I think you ought to take off,' he said on the telephone. 'For all we know the weather might clear just in time. In any case, the King will be witnessing the fly-past.'

'In which case,' I suggested, 'His Majesty is going to get bloody wet. Have you studied the met charts?'

'I haven't had the time,' he remarked crossly. 'I've only just got into my office.'

'Well, I've had time,' I told him, 'and I can say two things. First you won't get any contrails out of me. Next you'll have to cancel your fly-past. I'll bet you a fiver on this.'

'I'm not a betting man,' he replied primly. 'But I must ask you to take off at the pre-arranged time.'

When one is dealing with a maniac one has to soothe him, so we took off as arranged, hit cloud at four hundred feet, climbed on course to twenty-five thousand feet in thick and turbulent cloud and I then decided to abort the mission. Ground aids had improved since the earlier days and I rang up Heathrow Navigation Centre on the R/T and asked for homing assistance.

'I have you on radar, Blinker leader,' came a woman's voice over the ether.

'I don't want to talk to a bloody woman,' I replied. 'Give me the controller.'

'I am the controller, Blinker leader,' she replied.

'In which case I apologize in advance for the language you are going to hear,' I said.

'Now, now. Calm down,' she said soothingly. 'You are at twenty-five thousand feet over the Croydon region. Vector two two five degrees and commence your descent.'

'Bloody hell,' I snarled. 'You sound just like an old nanny.'

'Tut tut,' she replied. 'Inform me when you are at angels ten.'

I had no other recourse but to do what she said, and she was bloody marvellous. She dropped us out of cloud at about three hundred feet right over Brighton Pier, and the downs behind reached up to about eight hundred feet. I told her I was in visual contact with the ground, thanked her and said I would ring her up when we landed. We scorched along the Sussex coastline and the weather was deteriorating even further; it was difficult to distinguish between the grey of the sea and the grey of the cloud. I was flying at two hundred feet which meant that the trailing members of the squadron were stepped down to one hundred; I couldn't afford to fly any lower or I would have put the arse-end Charlies in the sea. We passed the pier at Worthing and then Selsey Bill loomed out of the rain; then I knew exactly where I was. I asked the airfield controller what runway was in use and he said it would be a landing from west to east which suited me very well in the conditions. I told him I wanted to make a straight-off landing and he then asked me if I could hold off as a squadron of Canadians were also asking for priority. I lied, said we were short of fuel and I was going to land come hell or high water. He had no alternative but to acquiesce.

We followed the distinctive road that leads from Selsey to Chichester, and at that moment I put the squadron into sections line astern, aircraft echeloned port. I dimly saw Chichester cathedral and started the turn for the final approach just before we arrived over it; one of the arse-end Charlies nearly removed some of the gargoyles. We made a neat enough landing on the main runway at Tangmere, taxied to the end of the runway and on to the squadron dispersal. I got out and waited for the Canadians to appear. By now the cloud was just about on the deck. They broke four aircraft on landing. Whoever ordered us off in those conditions should have been shot in the Tower of London. It was the most hazardous flight with a squadron hanging behind me I ever made.

When I got back to my office I rang up Heathrow Navigation Centre and asked to speak to the controller.

'You're the first woman I have ever trusted,' I told her over the telephone.

'But you should trust us women,' she said primly. 'We are very efficient.'

She was indubitably one of the most efficient women I have ever met.

Good old Clare!

Then they decided that we should convert on to jets, so our Spitfires were flown away and we were given Meteors Mark III. There was a slight difficulty in the conversion programme because no one on the Station knew how to fly the Meteor. I found one chap who had a passing knowledge and I sat in the cockpit while he told me what he knew about the taps which wasn't much. He did point out that the two jets took a long time to give the aircraft acceleration on the take-off run, so it would be necessary to get them up to full thrust before take-off, keeping the aircraft held on the brakes in the interim. The vital instruments were, he said, the temperature gauges and if they went off the clock it meant the aircraft would catch fire soon afterwards. The fuel gauges were also important as jets use an inordinate amount of fuel at low level and only developed efficiency at great height.

I was thus in a state of fair ignorance as I taxied out to the runway. The Meteor, of course, had a tricycle nosewheel undercarriage and one could see clearly ahead, a remarkable difference from the high-nosed Spitfire. Then there was the silence of the jets in the pressurized cockpit. Our modern Spitfires were also pressurized as they could fly just about as high as the Meteor, but the roar of the propeller broke the silence nevertheless. Next there was the noticeable absence of vibration. Although the jets in the Meteor rotated at thousands of revs per minute, six times as fast as the Griffon engine in the Spitfire Mark XXI, they did not also have to work to make an enormous propeller rotate in consonance, hence the absence of vibration.

I lined her up on the runway, clamped the brakes on and opened up the two jet engines – maximum revs were four-teen thousand five hundred per minute, as I recollect. The thrust shoved the Meteor forward against the brakes and when I released the brake lever she moved slowly up the runway reminiscent of the American Thunderbolt in which I had taken off from this very same runway years before. But as the air began to be sucked into the jet intakes she accelerated rapidly and when I sensed that she had gained flying speed I hauled her gently off the ground. She had needed 15 degrees of flap for take-off and the shorter of the two runways was in use at the time. This was fine for take-off as the flight path would be over the flat area towards the coast. She gained climbing speed quite quickly and the jets had been squealing like a stuck pig on take-off, but comparative silence descended when I began to climb at reduced throttle.

The Meteor was just an old carthorse compared with the Spitfire, with its twin engines, slow aileron control and sluggish reactions to movements of the throttle. Nevertheless, she was great fun to fly although I would have hated to fly this aircraft in combat conditions except when aiming at mindless targets such as flying bombs. But the Meteor was most certainly faster than the Spitfire Mark XXI and the faster I flew the more responsive became the throttles as great quantities of air were sucked into the intakes, heated to two thousand degrees celcius, expanded and hurled out of the effluxes. I played around with her at a safe height, looped and did a few vertical rolls, then I dived towards Tangmere. Air Traffic Control procedures were rather stricter than they used to be, so I called up the airfield controller and requested permission to beat up the airfield.

'Please give your reason,' he requested sternly.

'It's all to do with Meteors and morale,' I replied. 'In any case, I am coming in fast from the east. Be with you in thirty seconds.'

He was confounded but he hastily cleared the circuit, and I screeched over the squadron dispersal hut at 450 knots, went into a vertical climb, rolled her three times on the way up, half-rolled out and descended gently towards the runway having first extended the airbrakes which are essential to jet aircraft.

The short runway was all very well for the purpose of take-off, but on landing one had to pass over the downs at Goodwood which must be about four hundred feet high and were quite close to the threshold of the runway in question. So I left the airbrakes out, gave her full flap, and touched down slightly fast. No one had told me about the trick when landing jet fighter aircraft, which was to keep the nose up for as long as possible while running along the runway thus maintaining maximum drag and making the air itself a form of brake. Without this knowledge I plonked her down on her nosewheel much too soon, and she ran on like a hare being chased by a couple of lurchers. I gingerly squeezed the brakes and they seemed to have little effect so my problem became how to stop her before we ran off the runway. If I made too much use of the brakes, they would get red hot and lose their effectiveness. I was now in dire trouble as the runway threshold appeared to be getting closer every second. I sponged the brakes on, released them, applied brake again and hoped. She stopped a mere three feet from the ploughland beyond the runway. I taxied her back to the squadron very gingerly, making the least possible use of the brakes. They must have been white hot not just red hot.

I disembarked from the cockpit and my Senior Flight Commander was there to greet me.

'What are they like to fly?' he inquired.

'Oh it's just a piece of cake, old chap,' I replied nonchalantly.

'I thought it must be a piece of cake,' he remarked rudely. 'When I saw *you* do that upward Charley on your first solo, I thought it really must be a piece of cake.'

How insulting can one be?

EIGHT

MY FIFTH SQUADRON

WHEN the war ended, for economy reasons, the front-line of Fighter Command was reduced to cadre form, meaning that the establishment of squadron aircraft was cut by half. This was, in fact, a sensible policy as it retained the integrity of famous squadrons and gave facilities for a quick expansion of the fighter force if an international crisis loomed up. What this meant to me, however, was that I was no longer in command of a squadron, merely of a flight, so I opted out and in 1947 accepted an appointment as Air Defence Adviser to the Government of the Netherlands. The Dutch Air Force was in a horrible mess and, with great respect to my many Hollander friends, had hardly ever been an effective fighting force previously. It had had no operational experience in the First World War as Holland was neutral, and it had been wiped out in Metropolitan Holland in one day by the Luftwaffe in 1940.

I spent three years in Holland, and when I became accustomed to the Dutch way of life, I loved every moment of it. The dreamy canals have to be absorbed within the spirit not just glanced at. The architecture is worth a long visit to that country. The flat fen land brings in train a clarity in visibility which is almost unique in the world. This, of course, set the great Dutch painters working on their landscapes, and from those exercises there evolved pictures of the interiors of Dutch homes with the ornaments and costumes, the portraits, the self-portraits of geniuses such as Rembrandt and, in my view, best of them all, the superb paintings of my favourite artist, Vermeer. He made his own paints from minerals crushed with pestles and mortars, the whites of egg and so on. His blues, although 300 years old and more, have not yet faded. The only place worthy of hanging pictures by Vermeer is the Mauritshuis in The Hague which is surrounded by a moat. It is not possible properly to appreciate a Vermeer except in a Dutch art gallery.

When I had finished with my tour of duty in Holland, I went to the Air Ministry, to the Personnel department, to discuss my next appointment. The officer with responsibility asked me what sort of job I would prefer to have and I told him that I would prefer to take command of a squadron in Fighter Command, whereupon he lay back in his chair and giggled until foam came out of his mouth.

'What's so funny about that?' I inquired.

'My dear fellow,' he said, wiping his eyes with his handkerchief, 'you've already commanded more squadrons than almost any other individual officer since the RAF was formed. You haven't got a hope of another chance.'

'Incidentally,' this chap then informed me, 'Billy Bruce wants to see you while you're here. I'll take you along and we can fix things up later.'

Billy Bruce was an old friend of mine and equally important he was the Wing Commander with special responsibility for posting people like myself to flying appointments. I went into his office and he was lying back on his chair with his feet on the desk. He got up and shook my hand and we talked about old times. I then pulled off a superb confidence trick. Billy Bruce ate the bait and trundled me back to his subordinate's office. He told him to post me as commander of the squadron at Tangmere where there was a vacancy.

His subordinate gazed at Billy with a blank look in his eyes.

'But, sir,' he exclaimed, 'you can't give him another squadron – why he's commanded four already.'

'So what?' Billy inquired, and he and I went off to the pub for a drink – I paid.

I went home and in the course of time received a signal ordering me to report to Eleven Group Headquarters prior to proceeding to Tangmere, as the AOC wanted to interview me. I reported to the office of his Senior Air Staff Officer, knocked on the door, entered, and who should I find with his feet on the desk gazing at me with an enormous grin on his face but my old friend Jasper, my Squadron Commander during the Battle of Britain. I had met him only once since that time and he then tricked me into knocking down the wall which surrounded his house with my service car, partly on account of booze, mainly because of the tactics he employed to bring this about. I did not hurt myself but the car was a write-off.

'I heard you'd be around again,' he said, 'come to the mess and we'll have a drink.'

'But I am supposed to be interviewed by the AOC,' I protested.

'Don't worry. You can see him after we've had a drink.'

So we went to the mess, Jasper gave me four double gins, escorted me back and I rolled into the AOC's office tight as a fat girl's shorts.

The AOC was a very knowing man, and he also knew Jasper very well, so he gave me a kindly grin and suggested I sat down before I fell down. We had a very amicable conversation as he was also a one-time commander of the squadron I was going to command.

I arrived at Tangmere and was interviewed by the Station Commander, who is one of the finest men who ever lived and a rock-hard friend of mine today. He drove me to the squadron dispersal hut, introduced me to my new team. A

Meteor then overshot, vanished from sight and somebody yelled *'He's gone in!'*

I thought they meant that some dignitary or other had entered the squadron hut without my knowledge, so I sauntered into the shack, whereas the Station Commander, and everybody else who had been standing around, got into their cars and disappeared at high speed on the perimeter road of the airfield. I thought this was all very peculiar but decided to follow in another car which I hi-jacked. I arrived at the Station Commander's official house, continued further until I came to the rugby pitch. There, smoking, was a Meteor which had touched down on its belly and skidded to a halt almost exactly under one of the goal posts. It must have missed the house by only a couple of feet. Then I noticed that it had black and white chequers painted on the fuselage, and these represented the colours of the squadron I had just assumed command of – in theory if not in fact.

When I arrived back at my office the telephone rang and it was Jasper acting in his role as SASO Eleven Group.

'Congratulations, old chap,' he remarked. 'This must be the first ever.'

'The first ever what?' I inquired.

'The first time ever that a Squadron Commander managed to have one of his aircraft broken within five minutes of arrival in his new post.'

'In omnibus princeps,' I replied.

'And what the hell does that mean?'

'There's got to be a first time for everything.'

Jasper rang off in disgust.

As the pilot had not been killed in the accident no Court of Inquiry was necessary but I had to put in a report. I saw the pilot who was unhurt apart from a gash over his eye, but was clearly very shaken which was not surprising. With his assistance I worked out what had happened and he had been practising single engine flying on the twin engine Meteor Mark IV, had turned off one engine and it would not re-light despite his several attempts to make it do so. His only recourse, accordingly, had been to make a single engine landing. This required very nice judgement with the Meteor, which was gentle as a lamb on one engine unless full power was applied to it when the physical strength then required to maintain control in the lateral plane was almost beyond human ability. Although the pilot was experienced – had indeed been an instructor on Meteors – he made a grave error of judgement in this case.

It is comparatively easy to assess why a naval ship might wear an air of tradition: historically there might have been up to ten which bore the name *Hood*, for example. It is no simple task to comprehend why one RAF squadron is full of traditional values whereas another is not. For whatever reason, the squadron I had under command in 1950 and beyond, simply reeked of tradition. It hit me like a typhoon; it followed me everywhere; it even penetrated my dreams when I was supposed to be asleep. Our squadron insignia was a fighting cock, and coincidentally the brewery under the management of the company of Messrs Courage Ltd. had the same emblem. They played along with me and in no time at all the squadron rooms were littered with models of Courage fighting cocks. Next, as this particular squadron used to perform tied-together acrobatics at the Hendon Air Pageant in the 1920s, there came the need for an aerobatic team to be formed. We even made the attempt to tie the Meteors together for the purpose, but things were rather more complicated in 1950 than they were in 1926, so the idea had to be dropped.

Then after a few months at Tangmere a bombshell dropped on my lap when the Station Commander asked me to come to his office, sat me down and looked at me warily.

'You're not going to like this,' he said.

'What?' I inquired.

'Your squadron is going to have to re-deploy to Leuchars in Scotland.'

I stared at him with my mouth open.

'But that can't be,' I said. 'This squadron, apart from the war years, has been in Tangmere since 1926. No one can pull roots of that strength from under us.'

'I'm afraid they have,' he replied gloomily.

Despite my protests and string-pulling I had no recourse except to fly the squadron from Tangmere to Leuchars. But I determined that if we had to operate in Scotland we would out-fly every other comparable outfit in Fighter Command. The first thing to be done, however, was to sort the RAF Station at Leuchars out as it had until recently been a Coastal Command station, stuffy as they come, and needed to be transformed into a live-wire fighter station. So the first thing we did was to break the billiard table. Next, I threatened to strangle the Senior Air Traffic Control officer if he did not swiftly change his systems in the manner of the very much slicker performance demanded by fighter aircraft. He did not quite cotton on as to the fact that there was a slight difference between handling a flying boat with 17 hours endurance and a Meteor that landed with only about five minutes fuel left in the tanks.

Then I made another of my errors of judgement. It demands a very nice appreciation to produce the required dash and élan in fighter pilots and at the same time stamp out tendencies towards over-confidence. I had a dashing enough young Pilot Officer in the outfit, but I was watching him like a hawk because my instincts were shrieking in the terms that he was getting over-confident. He capped it one day by racing his Meteor off the line at high revs, thereby blowing over the ground equipment, removing the hats of some airmen and nearly breaking the window of my office.

I rang up Air Traffic Control, stopped him from taking off, had him in, tore a great number of strips off him, warned him that I was inclined to assess him as over-confident and that only one more demonstration of this kind would lead to disaster. He would be grounded and I would take every possible step to have his flying brevet removed and get him transferred to ground duties. This was, so to speak, his last chance.

He certainly didn't have another chance; he didn't have another anything.

Close to the airfield, on the sand dunes, we had a ground firing range useful for testing the cannon in the Meteors, even more useful, perhaps, to the frugal Scots who used to arrive in their hordes at night to pinch the spent cannon shell cases which were made of brass and worth a good sum of money on the metal market. We used the range about once a week and the Range Safety officer would drive out there with the ground crew early in the morning. The RSO was a friend of my Pilot Officer X, and had I been given the mind of either a prophet or a high-grade detective in the Pinkerton Agency, I might have averted a tragedy by taking full note of this friendship. On the other hand, if a chap has been given his last warning, one might reasonably have expected that he would conform.

Maybe, maybe not; but Pilot Officer X was detailed on the last shoot of the day not long before dusk. He finished his firing practice, indeed, he made several holes in the target. Then he flew out to sea, turned for the hut where his friend was packing up for the day, at full throttle and flying very fast and at sea-level to demonstrate a sensational beat-up. He misjudged his altitude and hit a sand-dune at about 450 knots and that was the end of him. The difficulty then became to salvage what bits of the aircraft were still available, and for that matter, what bits of him were worthy of being placed in his coffin. The tide rose and carried the wreckage out to sea only to push it back again the next morning.

For reasons too complicated to explain, we worked during week-ends and took weekdays off in lieu. Nevertheless Saturday night to us was a party night and my Senior Flight Commander, Freddie, was possessed of a good enough thirst, and no doubt he drank his quota one Saturday and later tumbled into bed in his house which was about ten miles from the station. He failed to turn up for duty on Sunday morning, and this was excusable as the north-eastern *haar* had covered the airfield with cloud down to a hundred feet, so there was no point in getting the aircraft out of the hangar. I sent the ground crews home with instructions that they were not to leave the Station in case the *haar* decided to return to Iceland and thus make flying possible – a most unlikely proposition in the light of the met charts. Freddie had no telephone in his house and had to rely on the services of the village policeman to relay to him urgent operational messages. Accordingly, I rang up the village copper, told him to fit in his visit with any other business, informed him in confidence that this was a leg-pull and that on no account was he to inform Scotland Yard of my message; but would he be kind enough to tell Freddie that war had been declared and the squadron must take off for Norway before lunch.

The copper did not quite understand the gist of my message and I have a nasty feeling that he might well have informed Scotland Yard, who would in turn have informed the duty officer in the Cabinet Secretariat, and it is not impossible that every Permanent Under-Secretary of State in the land might have got into their barouches that Sunday morning together with their top-hats and sped to their offices in Whitehall. I cannot vouch for the plausibility of this, but Freddie arrived at the squadron within a quarter of an hour, automatically donned his flying overalls, and came to me

144

with his bone-dome in his hand and asked me what was the course to steer for Norway. His eyes were not only blood-shot, they were also glazed, but knowing Freddie as I did I knew he would most certainly have made Norway intact.

'Relax,' I instructed. 'We're off to the pub.'

His wide mouth creased into a grin.

'Good idea,' he said. 'I feel like a drink.'

But he always turned up for duty ever after no matter the weather conditions.

We had to perform all the chores of a fighter squadron in peacetime conditions. We had, for example, to re-deploy to East Anglian airfields for occasions such as fly-pasts over London as we had insufficient range to make any such attempt direct from Leuchars. Due mainly to the rivalry and enthusiasm of my two Flight Commanders, together with the efficiency of my senior Flight Sergeant who was responsible for the maintenance of the aircraft in collaboration with me and the Flight Commanders, we all managed to make sense of the complicated business of planning the flying programme and began to shoot to the top of the charts in terms of the utilization-rate per squadron aircraft. There was a norm laid down beyond which it was impossible to go. We set a new norm at a previously unheard of level.

It is a great responsibility to command a squadron with such exceptional credentials as those possessed by the one I refer to, and I was very well aware of this. The visitors' book was filled time and time again with the signatures of distinguished visitors; the old ones were continually being placed in the archives and new books purchased. The squadron photograph album was filled in no time, sent down to the archives and the process begun all over again. I studied photographs of 1930 vintage and discovered that in those days the squadron flew a rather unusual formation in the form of a cross, so I decided that we should learn to formate in similar fashion. This required careful calculation and appreciation, as it would be simply not worthwhile if we killed a pilot in the attempt. More important than getting into this formation was getting out of it. At the start, after take off, we would fly in a formation which looked like this.

↑
Direction of flight
Red section
Green section   †   † 1   †   Blue section
†   † 2   †
†   † 3   †
†   † 4   †

Then I would order Blue and Green fours to adopt line astern formation on Red section. When they were safely in position, I would tell Blue and Green section leaders to remove themselves a safe distance away, put their aircraft into echelon starboard and port respectively, bring them up to aircraft line abreast, and then move into line abreast on Red Three. The formation would then look like this.

↑
Direction of Flight
†

†

† † † † † †

†

†

†

One could hardly change course more than five degrees in this formation without the certainty of a mid-air collision, so it had to be completed on the final run-in to the target when I was roughly on course. Breaking up was even more hazardous than joining this formation; but by careful drill we achieved it.

As part of his role a successful Squadron Commander must be a good exponent of public relations, so when we had managed to make the cross formation one hundred per cent effective, I rang up the editor of *Flight* and suggested he should send one of his aerial photographers to Leuchars and also write a piece on the squadron. In due course, there arrived an ageing gentleman who, in fact, had taken shots of the squadron in the original formation during the 1930s. We put him in the front seat of a Meteor Mark VII and displayed our cross formation to him in the air. When we landed I asked him if he was happy about it. He said he was unhappy. We flew a perfect cross formation, he explained, but for photographic purposes it was necessary to fake the formation as, for example, the aircraft in line abreast would have to fly in echelon if the film was to show in the manner of a perfect cross. I arranged for a blackboard to be provided and he drew chalk marks illustrating exactly how he wanted the formation flown to get the best results on film. He was a leading expert in his own right so I certainly did not argue with him.

We took off on another sortie with the photographer in attendance in the Meteor Mark VII and he took some perfect shots which came out in the exact manner we had previously been flying, although when they were taken, we were falsifying the book so to speak. *Flight* gave us a good write-up which enhanced our reputation.

We used to fly down to Acklington which is situated north of Newcastle where they had an armament practice camp with target towing aircraft for the drogues and all the paraphernalia of gunnery training. We normally enjoyed this exercise, mainly because the wives were left behind and we were footloose and fancy free. The local hotel bore the title the White Swan, but we named it the Dirty Duck, and we spent a lot of time there.

I had an officer pilot on the squadron whose mother was French and he had an English father. He had been educated in France and spoke broken English. He was a wizard aerobatic pilot, a raconteur, a very amusing man and I was deeply attached to him. He was killed after I left the squadron when giving an aerobatic demonstration of some magnificence, but he flew too low, his wing-tip struck the ground, his Meteor cartwheeled and that was the end of him.

But he was very much alive when we decided to travel in convoy to a miner's club where there was in process a Friday night dance; Acklington is surrounded by coal mines. At the dance Georges – his name – flaunted up to a table where several young ladies, miners' daughters, were sitting and invited the one who caught his eye to take to the floor for a waltz. She agreed, Georges got down wind, promptly raised her arm and took from his pocket a phial of Chanel No. Five scent. He sprayed her under both armpits and then contentedly took her around the dance floor.

We had a young Pilot Officer on the squadron at this time and I thought he needed to be gently introduced to sex if he was ever to become a good enough squadron pilot, as flying and sex have a strange affinity. I accordingly selected another miner's daughter, who looked both clean and willing enough, and introduced him to her. He took her on a trail around the dance floor. Georges was in a fit of chagrin having, presumably, failed to make the grade with his girlfriend who was by now reeking of perspiration and Chanel No. Five. He was also horrified as he thought I had made a rather good selection for my Pilot Officer which would have done him very well later – or, perhaps, he would have done her very well.

'*Mon Commandant*,' he exclaimed in broken English, 'you must not let 'im 'ave that girl.'

'Why not, Georges?' I inquired.

'Because, in ze first place, she is too good for 'im. In ze next place, she attracts me very mooch. Et, at ze arse-end, zo to spik, 'e will not do 'er joostice when ze dance finishes.'

'*Pas de travail*, Georges,' I said. 'Why I'll find you another one, just as good, for yourself.'

Georges beamed.

'You promise zat, *mon Commandant*,' he exclaimed, 'you reely promize zat?'

'*Oui*, Georges,' I replied, 'wiz my 'and on my 'eart.'

It was at this miner's club I gleaned the knowledge that there was a fighting-cock fancier living in the district; we had a bantam cock with the name of Cockie who was our squadron mascot. But I thought at this stage that we needed something more positive than Cockie; we needed good and true fighting-cocks and where better to lay hands on the breed than in Northumberland. Cock-fighting in England, and in most other places in the world, is illegal because fighting cocks are ferocious birds and it is said to be a cruel sport. I doubt if it is any more cruel than shooting pheasants, in fact, and I know quite a lot about both cockfighting and shooting pheasants.

While we were temporarily based at Acklington, I thought this would be a good place to find a decent fighting cock and make him senior mascot over Cockie's head. Accordingly, one Sunday morning, I found Bill Niblett's little miner's cottage, walked up the path and knocked on the door. His wife opened it, I asked if I could talk to her husband and she let me in. Bill Niblett eyed me suspiciously but

I managed to break the ice. I had a fair idea that the sport was still practised in places like Northumberland; but when I hinted at this, Bill, of course, strenuously denied any such possibility.

His white painted, single-storey cottage was spick and span from the outside, tidy and clean as a new pin inside. I explained to Bill that my squadron crest was designed in the form of a fighting cock, and I wondered whether he could assist me in finding a suitable bird which would then become my squadron mascot. Bill invited his wife to make me some coffee while he summed me up to make quite sure I was not a copper's nark.

When he was satisfied that I was what I said I was, Bill told his wife that he would be back in good enough time for Sunday dinner and walked me along a secret path to a secret field where there was an enormous hen-coop. He dragged out by the scruff of its neck the biggest fighting cock I have ever seen. His Northumbrian accent is impossible to set down in the form of the written word and more's the pity for that. It was gruff, coarse, guttural and tended to sound as if he was spitting at the very moment of speech. However, I will do my best to illustrate the way he talked.

' 'eer iss a bloody good birrd,' Bill said.

I looked at it. It was a bloody good bird, weighed about 10 lb. and had a ferocious look in its eye.

'Aye, Bill,' I replied. 'That's a bloody good bird all right.'

'Aye. But he's a verry strong birrd. He'll need three hens to keep him quiet.'

'Do you have three hens to keep him quiet?'

'Arrr,' Bill replied.

I gave him a cheque for a tenner, he lent me a big basket to carry the fighting cock with his mistresses to my car and I arranged for the basket to be returned to his abode in due course. I also wrote him a letter inviting him to become an honorary member of our squadron association and in the envelope I enclosed a squadron tie. We finished our armament practice camp, left the Dirty Duck with some reluctance, and flew back to Leuchars. I arranged to have a very large coop built for the fighting cock and his mistresses, the grass outside squadron headquarters quickly became covered with birdshit, and Cockie used evasive action to keep away from the deadly clutches of the senior squadron mascot by flying off and sitting on the squadron name-plate outside my office.

After this our squadron aerobatic team was selected as the best one available in the whole of Fighter Command, whereupon I was told to get the team ready to proceed to the summer festival at Cannes to put on an aerobatic display. My wife was about to have (another) baby and I thought it appropriate that I should remain *in situ* rather than enjoy orgiastic experiences in the South of France, so I detailed Freddie to fly the team, with a reserve pilot, down to Cannes and put on a good show. The team was given white overalls and the aircraft were burnished so heavily the duralumin was nearly worn through. He got them to Cannes in one piece, using a staging post by the courtesy of the French Air Force, where they put up a brilliant performance. The Mayor of the town wined and dined them, they no doubt indulged themselves in orgiastic experiences – Georges was a member of the team and I have not the slightest doubt that he so indulged himself – and they returned with a couple of bottles of Napoleon brandy which had been presented to me by *M le Maire*. I gave one bottle to the groundcrews and the officers drank the contents of the other.

Time was by now running out for me as I had commanded the squadron for well over two years and I knew that I would never have the opportunity of being given another similar command. At about this time we were informed that the Navy was holding a large scale exercise in the area of the Firth of Forth and we were ordered to make simulated attacks on their ships so that their anti-aircraft gunners could enjoy some practice against live targets. It was a small fleet with other NATO naval forces involved and I thought it would be a good moment to scare the pants off these sailors. I briefed the selected pilots as to their duties, and told them in essence that I wanted them to fly no lower than two hundred feet and on no account to attempt to emulate my antics. Then we took off, flew in battle formation to the area and made a simulated attack on the ships. I went in at sea level pulling up just high enough to pass over the rigging and I certainly saw at least one frightened sailor jump overboard in consequence.

When we were running short of fuel I ordered the squadron to return to base independently and in due course landed back at Leuchars. When I was back on the ground I saw one of my Meteors taxiing in with a great gash in the leading edge of its wing. The pilot was Johnnie, one of the chaps with sufficient, if not too much, élan for my purpose. He had hit the rigging, if not the mast of one of the ships with very considerable force. How he survived the impact I will never know, but I put my highly trained team of engineers on to getting a new wing from an old wreck and fitting it in the place of the one with a murderous hole in it. I tore Johnnie off a strip, not so much for being in disobedience of orders, more for making such a fundamental error of judgement, but he was a good guy and I allowed him to stay with the squadron.

Then I wrote out a signal to the Admiral in command of the naval exercise. 'Deeply regret slight incident involving one of your ships. But we must make exercises in peacetime as realistic as possible.'

I received in very short time a reply.

Slight incident my sea-boots. You took the secondary mast off a corvette. Six sailors jumped overboard but survived after artificial respiration. Many thanks for your vivid co-operation. We were terrified but not dismayed. You have 'drench'd our steeples, drown'd the cocks'. Come up and have a drink some time.

Admiral, NATO Force, Rosyth.

In the course of time I received another signal posting me to Headquarters, Fighter Command, to the Staff of the Commander-in-Chief. I was dined out before I left and we broke the piano after dinner although there was hardly any need to do this. Leuchars was by now a fairly well streamlined fighter station, far removed from its old Coastal Command traditions. It was nothing like as streamlined as Tangmere, of course; there never was another fighter station comparable with Tangmere and there never will be.

NINE

STAFF OFFICER

I was not new to staff work when I joined the C-in-C's Headquarters at Bentley Priory near Stanmore, and I rather enjoyed the chore, especially if one was able to assist the chaps at the airfields in any way. My job was on the Operations side; if I had been given an Administrative appointment I would have shot myself. The C-in-C had me in for a formal interview and he was about the toughest *hombre* on earth. He was erect, not particularly tall, and had the steeliest blue eyes imaginable. He also had a slightly embarrassing trait which was to move closer and closer to one which gave but two options: either to back away until one arrived at the wall, or to stand firm until his penetrating eyes were about two inches from yours. After a little practice, I tended to stand firm. He told me something which I had to remember if I was to stay on his staff; that he didn't give a damn whether I turned up in my office sharp at nine a.m., or whether I left at three p.m., or whatever; all he wanted from me was results and he cared not a fig how I achieved this. He pointed out that the bureaucracy in the Air Ministry did not work with such flexibility; but he reassured me that he didn't give a bugger about the Air Ministry, so I should not allow that to inhibit my working practices in any way.

I performed no miracles as a staff officer at Headquarters, Fighter Command, but the short time I spent there was enjoyable. My colleagues mostly had a background based on operational experience in fighters, we spoke the same language and we generally enjoyed life. Fighter pilots squeeze as much fun out of life as possible and they are – or were – a breed apart from any other social class in Britain, including bomber pilots, and most certainly civil servants.

But I did not last long as a staff officer at HQFC because I was promoted out of the job with the rank of Wing Commander and despatched to the headquarters of Eleven Group, as officer in charge of operations. If I had known then what I know today, I would have opted out, asked to be reduced in rank, and sent to be another of the academics who tend to inhabit the Air Ministry – even in an administrative job. Julius Caesar was invited to beware the Ides of March. I should have taken due note that I ought to have avoided being on the staff of Eleven Group as the end of 1952 appeared on the calendars; because 1953 was to be the year when the young Queen Elizabeth was crowned.

My immediate boss at Eleven Group Headquarters was the Senior Air Staff officer, Group Captain Tommy Towers, a man notorious for his asperity, but as fine a fighter pilot as they come and a very experienced wing leader. He was a perfectionist and used to get extremely excited when the officers of his staff failed to keep pace with his quick-moving brain. I served under him for almost exactly a year and we were the two hardest-worked officers in the Air Force; I had only one flaming row with him despite the exciting times we lived through, which showed commendable restraint on his part – and on mine for that matter. We proved to be a solid almost unbeatable team working under the light touch of the Air Officer Commanding Eleven Group, Air Vice Marshal Pat Brown. The AOC was one of the greatest characters in the RAF and was partly responsible for giving it the spirit of dash and élan which, alas, has now left it.

Pat had at one time been a flying instructor, and on one occasion decided to leave his rear cockpit and clamber out on to the wing of the biplane. His pupil pilot was concentrating on flying the aircraft and failed to observe the fact that his instructor was sitting gazing at him from about three feet away. So Pat laid hand on the aileron and waggled it, which meant that the joystick held in the hand of the pupil jumped around like anything. The pupil was startled by this phenomenon and raised his eyes from the instrument panel. When he saw his instructor sitting on the wing alongside him, he nearly spun the aircraft into the ground in terror. But that was the spirit necessary, that was the quintessence of the RAF in its halcyon days.

He had under his command possibly thirty RAF stations some of which contained squadrons of the Royal Auxiliary Air Force, and his radar stations extended from Suffolk to Cornwall. Being a man of considerable sagacity he made it a point to visit as many of his outlying units as he could, and most of them had never heard of, let alone met, their AOC before. To a man, the personnel of these units were invigorated by his visits and, in consquence, did a better job of work after he had descended on them and left later in a cloud of dust.

My job covered many facets and I could never have performed it effectively without the considerable experience of squadron work I had, by then, amassed. Fatal flying accidents, for example, occurred with desperate regularity at this period, due to lack of adequate navigational systems, sudden changes unpredicted in the weather forecasts and so on. On each occasion, the farce of the coroner's inquest apart, we had to establish Boards of Inquiry to investigate the cause of such accidents and these were normally headed by officers of at least equivalent rank to that of the Station Commander whose aircraft were involved. Such investigations were inevitably thorough and the written reports on the proceedings were sometimes verbose. Part of my duty was to read such reports with great care, and recommend what wording the AOC should use before he had a Board of Inquiry report despatched to HQFC, when the C-in-C would place his seal on the document before sending it to the Air Ministry.

Pat Brown came into my office one day puffing away at a cigarette as was his wont. His eyes contained a gleam of amusement and I knew he had something up his sleeve.

'Dizzy,' he said, 'I've just had a meeting with the C-in-C. We've cooked up a plan.'

'What's that, sir?' I inquired.

'Well, you know of course that the Queen is being crowned this year?'

I nodded in agreement.

'So there are going to be parades all over London by the Brigade of Guards, the Gurkhas and God knows who. Naturally in this light the RAF – especially Fighter Command – will have to do their stuff. On Coronation Day, for example, we will have to put an impressive fly-past over Buckingham Palace. Mark you, there's a bit more to it than just that.'

'Do you have any idea of the type of fly-past envisaged by you and the C-in-C?' I mildly inquired.

'Yes. I've drawn a plan. Here it is.'

He handed me a bit of paper with various squiggles drawn on it. I looked at it with blank amazement. This is how it was laid down.

'What, sir,' I inquired, 'is that supposed to mean?'

The AOC replied, 'It means six wings of Meteors with a squadron of F-84 Sabres in the middle. It's what we've decided to call a spearhead formation.'

'What, this massive number of fighters, in a cohesion formation, over Buckingham Palace, on Coronation Day, with a couple of million sightseers standing around the joint?'

'Yes. You've got the gist.'

I gazed at him with glazed eyes.

'Meaning I've got to plan this?'

'That's right. Furthermore, we cannot afford a single flying accident. If we had a mid-air collision over London, we might knock off a couple of thousand spectators.'

I grabbed at a piece of paper and drew the formation in detail. This is how it looked.

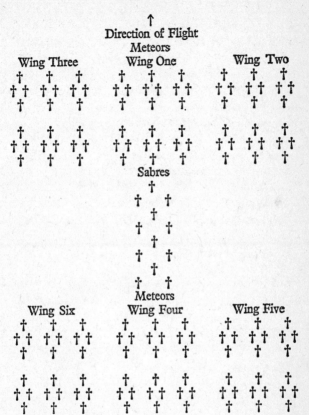

When I had drawn a detailed outline of the suggested formation, I handed it to the AOC. His eyes glazed over immediately.

'It's bloody well impossible,' I suggested.

He puffed away at his cigarette.

'If it is impossible,' he said, 'you've got to do the impossible. Anyway SASO will help you out. He knows what he is talking about; you can rely on him.'

My mind filled with horror at the prospect. The sheer technicalities began to rush into my head so I blanked off, because one needs time to consider operations of such magnitude and it is better to plan in the unconscious part of the mind, so to speak.

'Incidentally,' the AOC said, lighting up another cigarette, 'we've got another fly-past to plan this year, apart from that one and the other routine ones.'

'Such as what?' I inquired with some asperity.

'Such as we've got to put over Odiham rather more than 600 aircraft for the Coronation Review of the RAF by the Queen. All the commands in the RAF will have to be represented in this.'

I practically fell out of my chair.

'Come on,' he said. 'It will be all right on the day. Let's go to the mess and have a drink.'

And by God I needed it!

When dealing merely with the routine work as Officer in Charge of Operations at Eleven Group Headquarters there was enough, in all conscience, to be done when one takes into account the considerable number of squadrons under command at that time. But the infliction of two massive fly-pasts in addition made for an impossible situation unless one could manage to keep two paces ahead of events. So I requested the appointment of another three officers on a temporary basis to the staff which the Air Ministry immediately turned down. Whereupon Pat Brown, who appreciated the future problems very well, did his stuff and we squeezed another three Staff Officers out of the rock apes. Then I demanded another office which could be transformed into a map room and was given one. One of the new Staff Officers was, fortunately, a navigator and I set him up in his shop in the map-room. We had two major operations to plan both of which were unprecedented in the history of the RAF.

No one had previously made the attempt to join up about two hundred fighters in a cohesive formation of this nature, still less fly it over London when the city was packed with sightseers. We certainly could not have afforded a mid-air collision over the crowded streets. Further, planning means exactly what it says; if it were now February, we had to be ready to press the button on Coronation Day which was billed for May. No one could say what weather conditions would prevail on the day, so we had to work out a bad weather plan, which would take a completely different form from the massed fighter formation which the C-in-C and my AOC had decided to adopt.

A further complication was that this massive fighter formation must never be allowed to proceed on to London ahead of Coronation Day, as it had to be kept secret from the Queen; we wanted to give her a very special Coronation Day present, a sight she would have never seen before, nor had anyone else for that matter. Accordingly, whereas we would be able to stage full dress rehearsals up to a point outside the area of Inner London, we would never be able to rehearse the formation to its target – which was Buckingham Palace. It wasn't even Buckingham Palace: it was a point in space two hundred yards from the balcony of Buckingham Palace. This was so because, it was assumed, the Queen would be still wearing her heavy crown, hot from the Archbishop of Canterbury and Westminster Abbey. Our routing and planning would have to take this into consideration; she must on no account have to lift her head too high.

The next item of importance was that whereas the complex Coronation Day fly-past had to be planned well ahead of the moment, so did the even larger formation which would overfly the RAF Station at Odiham in June need to be given the full treatment within a similar time scale. Whereas the formation over Buckingham Palace would consist entirely of aircraft drawn from Fighter Command, which would facilitate the planning to some extent, the Coronation Review fly-past consisting of more than 600 aircraft, would involve almost every Command in the RAF. I went home to sleep on these projects and woke up in the middle of the night screaming.

The weeks passed, and apart from the routine work of keeping an eye on all the squadrons in the group and telling the staff at HQFC to go to hell, I spent most of the time doodling. Tommy Towers began to get impatient as he wanted proof positive that we could get the big fighter formation assembled. What I was more concerned about at this time was how could we plan to break it up again into individual wing formations without any mid-air collisions. But one day Tommy asked me to accompany him to the map-room and then inquired how did I propose exactly to form up all these aircraft. At that moment in time, in the front of my brain, I hadn't got the first idea, but as I walked over to the maps it all poured out from the subconscious mind as easy as easy.

We would use three Meteor wings, based in East Anglia, as the lead formation and they would join up in such and such a manner; the F–84s would come in behind and meet them at somewhere like Southend Pier; meanwhile, three Meteor wings based south of the Thames would be joining formation and the major point of rendezvous would be the city of Canterbury with its cathedral, a prominent landmark. They would stay in loose formation while the formation leader set course for Bexhill in Sussex, an easily identifiable turning point; they would have to stay in loose formation up to this stage as it was impossible, without risk of collisions, to change course more than a few degrees when this formation was tightened up. The total force would ease into tight formation having made their final major adjustment of course over Bexhill, and we would have to organize the finest navigational devices available to assist the leader on his final run-in towards London. We would break the formation up – very carefully – over Biggin Hill airfield on the rehearsals, but we would have to lay down flares on the ground for the tricky last lap through to Buckingham Palace on Coronation Day itself. This would be a final flight of about fifteen miles and we needed long burning flares placed at intervals of one mile on this route, to assist the leader.

The bad weather plan was a piece of cake after this – the fair-weather plan – had been agreed by Tommy. But there were still a number of most important details to be thought out, such as the best speed to fly, how to break the formation up over Biggin Hill during the rehearsals; worse, how to break it up safely after it had passed over Buckingham Palace on Coronation Day. Where would we establish our command post? And there were a further hundred factors which needed thought. Most important was the speed to be flown by the leader, as while making adjustments of course over such places as Bexhill, even when in loose formation, the wings on the inside of the turns would have to throttle hard back, and those on the outside would have to accelerate sufficiently to fly at some hundred knots faster than their colleagues on the inside during the turns. Another nice point was that when the wings made rendezvous, they must be approaching each other at gentle angles, because a single wing formation was unmanoeuvrable, whereas this monster formation comprising as it did three wings in the lead, one squadron in the middle and a further three wings in the van could hardly adjust course more than a couple of degrees; and even such alterations in bearing might have dramatic implications for some of the pilots flying in the squadrons of the wings.

However, having thought the whole thing through, we then sat down and wrote a thick operation order, had it roneoed and despatched to the airfields and ground stations concerned. We also invited one of the leading manufacturers of aerial navigation equipment to co-operate and the company brought out a prototype of a new navigation aid, set it up in a caravan, and we arranged for it to be sited in Regent's Park on a direct line with the planned approach of the formation. We set up similar devices at Biggin Hill to assist the formation leader on his run-in from Bexhill. Meanwhile, one of our attached Staff Officers was busy finding sites ranging from Biggin Hill to Buckingham Palace for our ground flares. The mineral water company, Schweppes, were kind enough to allow us to set up a flare site on the roof of one of their factories in South London and shortly afterwards wished they hadn't. When we tried one out on the roof, pungent smoke poured into their air intakes, mucked up the filterization system and ruined a production run of some three million bottles of 'Sch! You know who!' We moved that site to another factory when we appreciated the problem.

Honi soit qui mal y pense!

As the calendar moved on, we made final checks of our plans and Pat Brown ordered the first rehearsal; we were now moving from the theoretical to the practical and this was unknown territory. The AOC poled our ancient Anson in the vague direction of Biggin Hill, where we would break the formation up, the wing leaders would disassociate themselves from their formations, and we would all meet up to take note of the trouble and strife they would undoubtedly hand out to us at the debriefing. En route to Biggin Hill, the AOC overflew the criminal lunatic asylum at Broadmoor.

He pointed down vigorously and said:

'That's where I was educated.'

He thought it was Wellington College, not far up the road, where he had in fact been educated. Tommy and I told him we were absolutely certain that he had been educated at

164

Broadmoor because it showed. The AOC just grinned. And in this manner we arrived at Biggin Hill airfield which I had not seen for some thirteen years.

The basis of the formation plan depended on accurate and synchronized stopwatches and we had instructed the flying leaders to check their watches at a specific time with a particular Greenwich time signal as broadcast by the BBC. It had to be a selected time signal since we discovered, on one occasion, that the 'pips' were five seconds slow. This did not matter at all provided every leader's watch was five seconds fast, but our timing demanded an accuracy of five seconds. We had a mobile R/T set placed outside the flying control tower at Biggin Hill but we made no attempt to transmit any orders; the whole basis of the formation relied on the planning previously undergone and a strict adherence to our timetable. But we listened in as the wings made rendezvous over Canterbury, and then we heard the formation leader telling the wing leaders to close their formations as he turned on his final approach over Bexhill.

This massive formation, comprising some two hundred jet fighters, bubbled on the horizon, passed over our heads as we watched at Biggin Hill in a single second and made a noise like a young atom bomb exploding. Then there was an ear-splitting silence until the individual aircraft of the wing leaders joined circuit and landed. We met them in the briefing room and all hell was let loose. This formation was not only impossible, they said; the planning must have been achieved by some crazy mixed-up kid. Here they were at the stall; there they were almost exceeding the speed of sound. Why couldn't one of them, they suggested, he attached to Headquarters Eleven Group to write a decent plan. Did we not know that we were merely a bunch of rock apes? (I knew who the rock apes were – the wing leaders!)

But Pat Brown was bloody marvellous. He squeezed some sense out of them and agreed, for example, to a change in

165

the speed of the formation. Tommy and I kept shaking our heads as they gained more and more concessions; the AOC bent with the wind, but he knew what he was doing all right. We ran about half a dozen rehearsals over Biggin; on each occasion we listened to complaints about the plan made by the wing leaders and the AOC kept giving away concessions which meant we kept having to amend our master plan. Then, at the final rehearsal he had them all over the barrel. He stood up on the rostrum when the final complaint had been heard and addressed this hard core of highly experienced fighter pilots.

'Chaps,' he said, his face alive with a broad grin. 'This has to me been a most interesting study in human nature. As you know you all disliked the original plan; as you also know, I instructed my staff to amend it in accordance with your wishes. Indeed, this process has been continuing for the last several weeks.'

They nodded gravely. Poor old AOC they thought. Surrounded by his rock apes. How they sympathized with him for having such inept staff officers as his advisers.

'Let me now tell you,' the AOC continued, 'that I have examined the updated plan which contains your required amendments, reamendments and so on, and I have compared it with the plan we originally drew up. Do you know what conclusion I came to?'

They shook their heads lugubriously.

'Well I'll tell you. After several rehearsals you now want to fly this formation in exactly the same way as the original plan worked it out for you. *Per ardua ad astra*. And my poor bloody staff have had to cope even with some of your more inane requests. Good morning. See you on the day.'

Wherepon they shoved off to their respective airfields, wiser and I hope sadder men. The brooding eye does sometimes see furthest.

We ran the bad weather programme on a couple of occasions and we could allow this to overfly London as there was nothing particularly spectacular about it: bad weather and sensationalism don't go together. The plan was merely to fly individual units across the line of sight from the balcony of Buckingham Palace with a time separation of thirty seconds for each wing. Tommy and I would watch from the Mall, and from the balcony of the Palace, measuring whether the formations were two hundred yards from the balcony, or whether they committed the mortal sin of being fifty yards out of position. We decided to establish the AOC's command post on the roof of the Palace and our signals' staff co-ordinated the requirements with the GPO. We had a direct line to Westminster Abbey, at the end of which was an officer whose job was to survey the scene and give us accurate information as to the time when the Coronation procession started for home. We had observers with R/T sets along the route to monitor the progress of the procession, as the estimated time of arrival of the Queen and her entourage was quite essential to our ordering the wings into the air at the correct moment. At low level, our Meteors had an endurance of only about one hour and we could not afford to have them hanging about. Once the decision to order them off was taken it was irrevocable.

Early on the morning of Coronation Day we studied the met charts with dismay. A couple of hours later, we studied them again and with the utmost despondency. The country was covered by a dirty great low pressure system with associated fronts, and it was obvious to me that the fair weather fly-past was a *non est* and it was extremely doubtful if we could order even the bad weather programme to be implemented. In addition, it was simply peeing with rain at our Headquarters near Uxbridge, the skies were not only leaden but obviously very turbulent; yet we could not afford a mid-air collision on any account; but at the same time we dearly wanted to put our fighters over London as a salute to the Queen.

We were given lunch by the AOC in his house, he, Tommy and I piled into his official car and we drove to Buckingham Palace which we had, by this time, got to know all too well. We parked in the rear drive and walked through the rain to a back entrance, got into a lift and ascended. Our command post was merely a small wooden hut on the roof of the Palace with a telephone and a met forecaster standing by. The AOC had bought a new RAF cap for the occasion and I suggested that he take it off his head and put it under cover out of the pouring rain. He protested that he would thereby be improperly dressed, and I suggested that it was better to be so than have an expensive cap covered with gold braid ruined. I was also improperly dressed as I was wearing a naval duffle-coat against the rain; he placed his new cap under cover. He also kept sending some of the most experienced pilots in Eleven Group into the air to give him a full weather reconnaissance report in the hope that the weather might break. But break it did not. It was fairly obvious by now that the bad weather programme could be implemented, absolutely certain that our carefully planned enormous fair weather fly-past would be quite impossible to achieve without putting London and its citizens in dire danger.

The AOC deferred his decision until the last possible moment, and his task was made no easier as the charts of the met officer became more and more sodden with rain and the isobars, accordingly, ran into each other. Then he dismally conveyed the message over the R/T that the bad weather plan would have to be put into operation. We were not yet out of the wood, however, as the Coronation procession was delayed at the Abbey and we had to hold our chaps on the ground until the required *moment critique*. At about this time the needs of nature overcame me and I disappeared

168

behind an appropriate chimney on the roof of Buckingham Palace. The AOC was by now jumping about a bit, and small wonder as he had been having a difficult time. So when I returned to the command post he inquired with considerable asperity where I had been and why I had deserted my post.

'I had to go and have a piddle, sir,' I replied.

'Where did you piddle?' he inquired.

'Just behind the chimney over there,' I told him.

'But you can't piddle on the Queen's roof!' he yelled.

'Sorry, sir. I have.'

He grumbled about this until he thought he too needed a piddle whereupon he made use of exactly the same chimney as I had done.

Then the Coronation parade turned up, and it was an unforgettable sight. The best part of it was watching the Air Staff trying to ride on horseback; they all kept on but were always at the point of falling off. We estimated that the wing should take off at a newly calculated time in view of the delay at Westminster Abbey, and the AOC gave the executive order for the bad weather programme to be set in train. When the first formation was turning over Bexhill and was a mere ten minutes away from its target, I rang up the robing room in the Palace and talked to an equerry who had a hole in his head and didn't understand what I was trying to say.

'Get the monarch out on the balcony bloody quick sharp,' I said, before I eventually put the telephone back on its hook.

We could not see the balcony from our position on the roof but the roar from the tens of thousands of people standing round the Palace gave us the intelligence that the Queen and her entourage were there. She arrived on the balcony with only a few minutes to spare and then the first of our wings flashed past precisely two hundred yards from the balcony; the rest followed at thirty second intervals. A bloody marvellous chap was my AOC. It was, after all, his responsibility not mine. I was just acting as a kind of planning ponce.

TEN

THE DAY I SOLOED THE SWIFT

WE had managed successfully to organize a massive fly-past over Buckingham Palace on Coronation Day in filthy weather conditions, but we were by no means out of the wood. We were, by now, a tighter-knit team but there was an even bigger project on our hands in the form of the Coronation Review fly-past. Whereas the Brigade of Guards, for example, have trooped the colour on numberless occasions on the Sovereign's birthday and, accordingly, have all the files handy stuffed with precedents, the RAF had never previously been reviewed by the monarch in a coronation year. The nearest occasion was during the Silver Jubilee celebrations for King George V, but on that occasion, in about 1936, biplanes were in squadron service and in that event the planners were able to redeploy the total force engaged for the fly-past on to a couple of airfields. In our case in 1953 there were no precedents whatsoever. My immediate impulse was to attempt to confine the Coronation Review fly-past only to units of Fighter Command as this would have simplified the planning task considerably. The AOC agreed in principle but doubted very much whether this would be possible. How right he was! Every command in the RAF wanted to be represented and most of the units outside Fighter Command didn't know the difference between flying in close formation and playing skittles.

Flying Training Command, for example, wanted to be in on the act with a formation of Chipmunks flying at one hundred mph, whereas the finale to the fly-past would be a Swift flying at six hundred knots. Bomber Command, who could hardly fly for toffee in close formation wanted their squadrons to adopt a difficult type of formation which they could never have achieved, so we had to talk them out of it. Coastal Command units would operate from places like Lossiemouth in the North of Scotland, Pembroke Dock in West Wales, and Londonderry in Northern Ireland all flying on converging courses. Then we had to negotiate with the test pilots who would be flying the prototypes of the Valiant, Vulcan, Victor, Javelin and Swift. Somehow, he had to congregate this mass of aircraft in orderly sequence in time and space over Odiham, and as they would be flying a course from North to South they would infringe London Airport's air traffic patterns.

It was all right on the day, however, just as Pat Brown had prognosticated. Visibility was excellent although the air was turbulent. I did the commentary over the Tannoy and they gave the Queen a decent enough lunch ahead of the moment. The timing overall, on the day, showed a mean error of 10 seconds for formations comprising 615 aircraft. Why, we even managed to educate Bomber Command!

As this hectic year dragged to a close the AOC asked me to come and see him in his office. I arrived and he looked at me with a gloomy eye.

'They say you've got to go to the Staff College?' he said.

'What's the purpose of going to the Staff College?' I inquired.

'Damned if I know. Supposed to make you a Staff Officer or something.'

'But I am a bloody Staff Officer, sir,' I reminded him. 'So

why waste the money on giving me a quite unnecessary course.'

He lit up another cigarette.

'In which case,' he inquired, 'why did you bother to take the entrance exam for the Staff College?'

'But that was just a form of insurance policy. In any case I didn't want the rock apes who inhabit the Air Ministry to think I was a bloody fool.'

'But Dizzy,' he said, 'I happen to know you're a bloody fool. My main task since you've been on my staff has been to keep that fact secret from the Air Ministry and, indeed, other authorities. If you don't do the Staff College course, they will know absolutely that you are a bloody fool. If you do it, they will have proof positive that you are a bloody fool.'

'OK, sir,' I said. 'I'll go.' So I went.

I will glide over my year at the RAF Staff College which was then based near Bracknell in Berkshire. This would be prudent as I might otherwise find myself being sued for libel. The only good occasion I seem to remember was when we once went down to Old Sarum to learn the intricacies of Army/Air support operations. Coincidentally, the annual fair was being held on the market square in the ancient city of Salisbury which we, naturally, attended. We entered the tent where the stripper would be divesting herself of her clothes and the *moment critique* came when she defiantly flung her brassiere onto the floor and I gazed at her boyish breasts with loathing. (If she had exposed her G String I would, without doubt, have vomited.)

In a loud voice a pal of mine expostulated:

'But we've got bigger tits than those on our directing staff!' How right he was.

I was appointed to the Joint Planning Staff based in the Cabinet Offices in London after I quite fortuitously graduated from the RAF Staff College. It took a whole year to become productive on the JPS, as worthwhile contributions depended absolutely upon a conditioned mind. Part of the conditioning process was to read, and furthermore understand, the views of about a hundred British ambassadors and British Commanders-in-Chief in overseas theatres, who operated from the ends of the earth and also reported daily. On the other hand, when one had managed to attain productivity, one also tended to become prolific. At which stage, the Secretary to the Joint Planning Staff came into our office one day and said that the Chiefs of Staff Committee wanted our appraisal of the strategic importance of Christmas Island and would we get a move on. My Naval and Army colleagues told me it was my turn to write the preliminary draft and this was a quite different assignment because we had no maps worthy of the name in our smoke-ridden office nor had the rest of the Joint Planning Staff for that matter, and I didn't know where Christmas Island was situated.

However, on reflection this seemed to present no special difficulties as Christmas Island had recently been the target for testing British nuclear bombs. When I got home I turned up my personal atlas and found out where Christmas Island was, calculated the weight of effluent left by the seagulls at the moment the nuclear bomb exploded above them, decided to inquire of the Whitehall Ministry with responsibility how much seagulls' effluent was now left there and went to bed without the need to wake up in the night screaming. The next day I wrote a crisp strategic appraisal as to the value of Christmas Island, my naval and army colleagues crossed the Ts and dotted the Is, we had a drafting session with our superiors and they sent the paper up to the Chiefs of Staff Committee for consideration at their next meeting.

A few days later, the Secretary to the Joint Planning Staff

stormed into our office with a puce face; I also took note that his eyes were bloodshot.

'You're a bunch of four letter words,' he expostulated.

We gazed at him with mild eyes.

'Why?' we asked in unison.

'Because you wrote an appreciation on the strategic importance of the *wrong* Christmas Island! Didn't you know there were two islands with the same title?'

'No,' I said. 'Did you?'

He lowered his head in dismay.

'No I didn't,' he explained. 'For that matter nor did the bloody Chiefs of Staff committee. They were about to put their seals on your paper when some geographer or other appreciated that they had been talking about the other one, not the one they were interested in.'

'So you can hardly blame us,' I suggested, as I took out my atlas, which I had prudently stuck in my brief case, in order to find out where the other Christmas Island was. This one was really covered with sea-gulls' effluent, which gave it its real strategic importance as it makes for good manure.

In retrospect, I enjoyed my two and a half years on the Joint Planning Staff; it gave one a good idea of the workings of British government. But as my tour of duty dragged to an end, I realized that I had been kept away from aircraft – apart from occasional flights intended to keep one mildly in flying practice – for nearly four years. Accordingly as the time arrived when I was due to be posted in about three months' time I machinated myself into another flying appointment, which was as Officer in Charge of Flying at a large RAF station in Germany.

My job in Germany can be best likened to that of airport manager which in the military genre was about the craziest setup I had ever experienced up to that time. I had no command responsibility over the squadrons based on the airfield in theory, although I could declare the airfield '*Red*', meaning unserviceable, because of weather conditions, or depending on the depth of snow and so on. I could not *order* the Squadron Commanders, who were of equivalent rank to myself, to give me their aircraft so as to keep myself in flying practice, only *invite* them to lend me aeroplanes as and when available. However, as there were four squadrons on the airfield, as the one Squadron Commander did not necessarily know when I was last lent an aeroplane by his colleagues, I got by to my satisfaction. I also had the Station Flight aircraft under my personal command.

The position improved considerably when they deployed a maintenance unit to the station with responsibility for performing major servicing on all the aircraft in the Second Tactical Air Force, because there were then a great variety of aircraft types in Germany. This unit also had its personal test pilot who was about the only man in Germany who was competent to fly this wide variety of aircraft. As I was the airport manager, he therefore came under my aegis, so I asked him to come and see me. His name was Paddy McArthur and he was a pretty wild Irishman.

'Paddy,' I said when he was comfortably seated, 'what happens to your testing programme when you go on leave, or go sick and things like that?'

'Nothing,' he replied. 'The test programme is held up until I get back to the unit.'

'Seems a bloody silly system to me,' I said. 'I'm sure that ICI, for example, would not allow their production lines to dry up just because one man was absent.'

'Yes, I take your point. But the trouble is that we have so many different types to test fly that there simply isn't anybody else in Germany who could act as my *locum tenens*.'

'Yes there is,' I told him.

'Who?' he inquired.

176

'Me,' I suggested.

His eyes goggled.

'But you can't do that! Don't you realize that it takes a three-month course to qualify on the Hunter – similarly with the Javelin and the Swift? That would mean that you would be away from the station for nine months simply getting the angles on just these three types for a start.' He scratched his head. 'I suppose you could test the Canberra and Meteor variants as you are qualified on both.'

'Bullshit,' I said. 'I fly by the seat of my pants. I hereby appoint myself as your deputy test pilot to the maintenance unit.'

Paddy sighed and his face contained a look of utter despair.

'OK, sir,' he breathed. 'Come down to the hangar and I'll show you the form.'

I had, of course, considerable flying experience on a great number of different aircraft. But I was never technically inclined, so I was a 'ham' test pilot. By this stage of the game, however, they had things called Blue Books in which were contained such technicalities as how to start up the relevant aircraft's engine, what its handling characteristics were, what speed it preferred to attain before being hauled into the air, and most important, what its approach and landing speeds were. Paddy gave me a bundle of Blue Books and I studied them later, but quickly appreciated that there was little point in any such exercise unless I was sitting in the cockpit. So I made a few inquiries, discovered that Paddy was due to go on leave in a few days time and that a batch of Hunters would require air testing in his absence. Accordingly I called on him in his office in the hangar which was furnished with a desk, a flying clothing locker, a couple of chairs and nothing else except a table on which were stacked about twenty Blue Books.

He gave me a mug of tea and wondered what the hell I

wanted so I told him. I said he might as well show me the taps on the Hunter before he went on leave as I would be flight testing the batch that was due to come off the line while he was absent. He gave in gracefully, took me to a Hunter in the hangar, saw me up the ladder into the cockpit, followed me and using the Blue Book as a form of interpretation showed me the taps. I stayed in the cockpit after he had departed down the ladder thumbing through the Blue Book and attempting to memorize all the intricacies of the instruments, warning lights and switches. I test flew my first Hunter the next day and adopted my ancient technique when flying completely strange aircraft. The most important facet of this was to make a simulated take-off by giving the engine full power and thus getting the aircraft rolling, then immediately closing the throttle which allowed her to cavort towards the end of the runway; whereupon one taxied gently back to the hangar. This gave a first class impression of the important aspects of take-off although, of course, one could only get the feel of handling a single seat aircraft in the air after a proper take-off; and one never knew how to land it until one had made the first landing.

It all worked very well and I test flew several Hunters while Paddy was on leave. Then a Javelin which needed to be test flown came on the line and Paddy, on his return, reluctantly agreed to allow me to make the flight the next morning. When the moment was due I climbed into my flying kit, the door of my office opened and in came the Station Navigation officer who was on my staff. He was dressed in flying kit.

'Where d'ye think you're going?' I inquired.

'I'm going to act as your navigator when you fly the Javelin this morning.'

'But I've never flown a Javelin before, you silly chap,' I said.

He beamed.

'*In omnibus princeps,*' he stated, well knowing that it was an expression I often used.

'Now look here, Bert,' I said. 'It's all very well for me to play silly buggers and take strange aircraft into the air for the first time without being officially qualified and all that. It is quite a different thing for me to risk someone else's neck through my sheer ignorance of the type. So you can't come along with me.'

'But you can't fly a Javelin without a navigator,' he pointed out. 'The centre of gravity will be all wrong for a start.'

He was having me on and I knew it. I took the Javelin up without him.

Paddy rang me up one day and said he wanted to 'rogue' a Meteor and would I fly it to confirm his suspicions. The implication of roguing an aircraft is that it is then placed 'Category 3 unserviceable', which automatically means that it is sent away for scrap. This is an expensive decision to take on an aircraft which is perfectly sound in all respects as far as the ground fitters are concerned and is a decision which is immutable when taken by an experienced pilot. Paddy was experienced enough, and if he said this Meteor was a rogue, I had confidence in his judgement, but he was too junior in rank to be allowed to send an expensive aircraft to the scrapyard.

I have declared probably more than a dozen aircraft 'rogues' in my RAF career. It is impossible to define a rogue as this depends on the intimate details of its handling characteristics in the air. If an aircraft feels unsafe, it normally is unsafe – but why? This might have been brought about, for example, by a heavy landing which distorted certain loadbearing members. Or if a wing had been removed on a major inspection and suffered stresses for unknown reasons whilst propped up against the hangar wall, and in all innocence replaced with even only a few millimetres of distortion, that might have been the cause, and so on. There is – or was – no engineering method capable of diagnosing the fault which could, therefore, only be exemplified by the handling characteristics in the air – slight though the defect might be in terms of engineering.

I opened the throttles and took off in the Meteor. I blanked out of my mind Paddy's interpretations describing his suspicions that she was a rogue in an attempt to remain as dispassionate as a high court judge. She wasn't guilty until I personally had found her to be so; in any case, as was usual, he had been unable to give any specific explanation. She behaved quite normally on the climb and at height. She aerobated normally, I extended the air brakes for the descent and she was perfectly stable when they caused the airframe to judder. She was fine on the circuit and I gave her a few degrees of flap as we were down-wind prior to the final approach. I made the turn at the normal speed for the final approach and then had a sick feeling that she was going to flick into a spin as the turn progressed. This was a purely instinctive reaction, there was no aeronautical logic in it; it was the sixth sense flashing red warning lights in my mind's eye.

I gave her more power, but the feeling persevered and I was hesitant whether to select flaps fully down as I straightened out with the runway directly ahead. I gave her full flap and trusted her not an inch. I kept her fifteen knots above the normal approach speed and waited tremulously for an incipient spin to occur at two hundred feet from the ground. When I was ten feet above the runway at much too high a speed, I gave her full air brakes and shut down the throttles. She dropped like a stone and I didn't care too much whether the tyres burst or not because my hand was on the undercarriage lever and I would have selected *Up* and sprawled her on her belly. The consequent damage would have been of no material importance because she was going to be sent off to the scrapheap in any case. Paddy was quite correct with his prognosis; she was a rogue all right – quite unfit for any further flights.

I called on Paddy MacArthur in his office having heard he had to go to London for an interview with the Air Ministry.

'What have you got coming up for testing?' I asked.

His face went green with despair and he clasped his hands together as if indulged in deep prayer.

'A Swift,' he groaned.

'OK. I'll test it as you're going to be away for a time.'

'Look, sir,' he pleaded, hands still clasped together. 'You simply cannot take the Swift off without a proper conversion course. It's an absolute bitch.'

'All aircraft are bitches unless they are handled right.'

'I know that. But there's never been a bitch like the Swift. For example, she drops like a brick shithouse on the approach if she loses just a little bit of power.'

In the event and with the greatest reluctance, Paddy showed me the taps in the Swift and then caught a flight to London.

The boss of the maintenance unit rang me up the next morning and told me that the Swift was on the line ready for air test. I pulled on my flying overalls, carried my bone-dome to the car and drove to the hangar. I told the Unit Commander that my intention was first to make a simulated take-off and then to taxi back. Would he arrange for the fuel tanks to be topped up on my return as that would give me time to think about the problem of the Swift before I later took it into the air?

'Make sure you don't lose the Blue Book,' he said. 'You'd be snookered if you lost the Blue Book. No one else on the Station knows how to fly the Swift, so there would be no help forthcoming over the R/T. You'd be on your own.'

'Bloody right,' I said, being in whole-hearted agreement with him.

The Swift was a military failure in design and this was probably due not so much to the maufacturers but to the rock apes in the Air Ministry who wrote the specifications. It was supposed to be an interceptor fighter and wasn't, so its role had to be changed to a fast, low-flying reconnaissance aircraft. It was a heavy single-seater aircraft which needed reheat to get it off the ground. Reheat is a process whereby additional kerosene is shot into the engine in enormous quantities on demand, while the engine is already roaring. The extremely high rate of fuel consumption involved in propelling the aircraft off the ground, and at low altitudes in the air, was about trebled with the application of reheat.

After making a simulated take-off and having returned to the hangar area, I clambered out as the mechanics approached with the refuelling bowser to top up the tanks ahead of take-off, walked away and smoked a cigarette while I studied the Blue Book once again. She was a fairly hairy bitch I considered, having taken her along the runway, and the prospect of flying the Swift solo for the first time was not made any more pleasurable because I did not really understand all the various emergency drills. All I knew in detail was how to pull the handle which would work the rocket-propelled ejector seat. I had done that only once before when I was shot up in a tower at the Martin Baker factory where ejector seats were manufactured, and the sheer forces, despite the precautions which I took, had probably caused a couple of my vertebrae to coincide; they are supposed to be maintained in an adjacent position, not quite touching each other, as two of mine seemed to be after my practice ejection.

However, when the mechanics had filled the fuel tanks and taken a quick look round the aircraft in case of any obvious unserviceability, I climbed aboard again, got the engine running as per the Blue Book, and taxied gingerly to the take-off point on the runway. I made the final checks as set out in the Blue Book, placed the document carefully on a ledge by the windshield, flicked down the switch which controlled the boost-brake and this locked the aircraft's brakes solidly on. I eased the throttle open to full revs, and the aircraft shuddered under the forces. Then I flicked the switch which operated the reheat. Even in the sealed cockpit the noise was appalling, and the Swift shuddered like an old maiden lady who knows she is shortly to be raped. Only the fact that the brakes were locked solid stopped her from making up her own mind that this was the moment or commencing the take-off run. Then I released the brakes, switched off the boost brake system and she trundled slowly at first, being a very heavy aircraft, up the runway. But she soon gained speed and then began to accelerate under the sheer forces of thrust. The air cooling system began to work with a vengeance as she arrived at take-off speed and dust blew into my eyes. The force of air entering the cock-pit promptly blew the Blue Book off the ledge and it glided to a halt somewhere on the floor between my boots. I was too busy hauling her off the ground to think about anything else at the time. However, when we arrived at one thousand feet I bent down to feel for the all-essential Blue Book; I felt nothing. I gazed down and saw that it was lying near my boots which were kicking away at the rudder bars, unlocked my safety harness, and stretched forward as far as I could. My gloved hands were still about six inches away from the Blue Book. It was impossible for me to reach it even at the extremity of my tremulous fingers. *Jesu Cristo y por el amor de Dios!*

I relaxed and managed to get the safety harness done up

once again, thought about using the ejection seat mechanism at this point, decided not to, and then concentrated on the instrument panel. The air speed indicator was showing a speed of six hundred knots, the fuel gauges were indicating less and less fuel availability every second, the reheat system was still working which should never have been allowed to happen, but, fortunately, I had remembered to retract the undercart else it would by now have been torn off. Further to this, I was flying very fast over flat, featureless, Dutch terrain and, indeed, I could see the North Sea ahead. I was utterly and completely lost and even at this stage I didn't have too much fuel left.

In my experience, on such occasions first things come first, so I switched off the reheat system, throttled back and turned the Swift on a reciprocal heading. I gained height to fifteen thousand feet to extend my range of vision and also to assist in cooling down the speed of the Swift from six hundred to about three hundred knots. I saw the River Maas ahead and then knew where I was. I spent just a little time giving her a flight test and called up the air traffic control tower to inform them that I was going to make a simulated landing, overshoot from it and then come in for a final landing. I kept my voice down to calm, clear speech as I didn't want them to know that I was sweating like a pig with sheer fright. They said that they would clear the circuit and keep it clear until I finally landed; I wondered if I ever would.

I put the undercarriage down at two hundred knots which, as I vaguely recollected from the lost Blue Book, would not necessarily mean that the landing gear would be torn off the aircraft on account of wind speed. Then I gave her first fifteen degrees of flap, and shortly afterwards full flap. She began to drop like the brick shithouse that Paddy had warned me about. I gave her full throttle to recover the situation and glanced anxiously at the fuel gauges. The fuel position was not too bad but was certainly not ideal. The final landing would be a do or die operation in terms of either a sufficiency of fuel to land or running dry on the final approach. Then I switched on the reheat system which was essential for an overshoot. Nothing happened, so I switched it off and on again in desperation. Still nothing happened. I now had on full throttle which gave insufficient power, was at a dangerously low speed, at a terrifying low altitude, in a bitch of an aircraft which had gone unserviceable on me in the air.

I gently hauled her up to gain altitude, simultaneously retracted the undercarriage and, in the course of time, the flaps. I simply did not have enough power and she remained staggering just above the stall. I fiddled with the reheat system but it would not operate, so I rang up the Tower over the R/T and told them that I was coming in for an emergency landing. I saw the fire engines trundle away from the fire station and the white ambulance arrived to join them at the upwind end of the runway shortly afterwards. They all positioned themselves in a strategic position from whence they could spray my burning body with foam and then put the debris in a jampot. The Swift staggered round the downwind turn just above stalling speed – but the stall arrives the sooner when one has put a wing down on a turn. I had managed to ease her up to about a thousand feet, and then gained adequate flying speed as I began to loose height on the final – the ultimate – approach. I lowered the undercart, and waited before giving her full flap. She began to drop but I held her up with increased engine power. Then I realized that I didn't know what her landing speed was because the Blue Book which contained that information was still lying passive beyond my reach.

I was totally committed to landing by now, so I put down full flap and increased the engine power. I touched her down at 150 knots and wondered whether the brakes would burn out before the tyres exploded with the heat. She touched the runway dainty as a virgin and trundled to a halt just before we ran on to the ploughland. I manipulated my handkerchief out of a pocket, and wiped the sweat from my brow; this also gave the brakes time to cool down.

I taxied her back to the hangar, slow as a model T Ford, and brooded en route.

The boss of the maintenance unit climbed up the ladder to help me get the safety harness undone.

'I was sitting in the caravan watching when you landed,' he said. 'I thought you pulled off a perfect landing, one of the best I've ever witnessed.'

I yawned.

'It's really a piece of cake, Charlie,' I replied. 'Any bloody fool can fly the Swift – provided he knows enough about aeroplanes.'

'Good show,' he said. 'We've got another one for testing tomorrow. Do you think you can manage the job?'

I could have cut his hand off. But it wasn't so bad the next time because the reheat worked all right.

Then I decided to give up my career as a pilot. I was, after all, getting rather long in the tooth. Indeed, seven years before this, when I was posted from command of my last squadron, the squadron personnel had presented me with a silver cigarette case. Inside they had inscribed on it: 'To sir, from all the chaps, on the occasion of his being posted to a desk. There is wisdom in this, much as he might dislike it. For sir is no longer a chicken.'

ELEVEN

EPITAPH TO *AER*

THE arts of airmanship are profoundly complex, more so even than those involving seamanship. This was certainly true in the period of my flying career, but modern navigational aids, radio communications, landing aids coupled with automatic pilots have today made the process itself almost automatic. The factor which was overriding during my time as an aviator was instinct born of experience. The foremost quality required to be a totally effective flying leader was based on total supervision. Flying accidents in the Royal Air Force were due on eighty-five per cent of occasions to lack of supervision; pilot error mainly filled up the residue. Pilot error was, of course, also part of the eighty-five per cent, but if one sent off a pilot on a mission for which he was inadequately trained, that amounted to lack of supervision. The thin line between producing the verve, dash and élan required in a fighter pilot, as opposed to the sin of over-confidence, demanded an almost magical ability to supervise, because judgement is part and parcel of supervision. Knowledge of men, of human nature, enters the argument; to fix on a pilot who lacks moral fibre before he flies away in retreat when the enemy appears requires a working knowledge of both aero-medicine and the teachings of Freud. Supervision must be overall to be effective; aircraft engineers can be the cause of flying accidents if they do not do their work effectively; air traffic controllers should be supervised by practising pilots, who in turn should understand the complications of ground control systems as well as they understand the arts of airmanship. The whole problem can be summed up in the word instinct.

Fundamental to airmanship is the ability accurately to forecast the weather prospects even without the use of meteorological charts. On one occasion the met forecaster was informing my squadron that the weather was set fair and that it would be a blue day. I was looking out of the window and I saw light snow falling. I pointed this out to him and he was confounded. Looking out of the window is the best possible manner in which to forecast the weather, providing one is well enough qualified to understand what the cloud formations portend. Met charts are, let it be said, useful documents provided one has the ability to read between the isobars. On one occasion, when I was planning a massive fly-past, the met forecaster – a man who was well above the average in his craft – gave his opinion that the weather would be good enough for the purpose at the planned time. I told him this was not so. The Meteorological Office was, at this period, based on Dunstable and he informed me that the whole weight of his mighty *apparatus* confirmed his opinion. I said that if we put the rehearsal for the fly-past in train, all our aircraft would have to be recalled long before their target was reached and a dangerous situation would materialize. I was in no position to take the fundamental decision to launch the several hundred aircraft involved; but those in authority decided pro the met forecasters and anti my own views, so the operation was started. In the event, we had to recall all the aircraft and order the pilots to return to their bases long before they reached their target, and a dangerous situation did indeed materialize. Dunstable had omitted to look out of the window.

On another occasion, when my squadron was based on

Around £13,000 can make your retirement as carefree as this.

It's very easy to make sure of a happy and secure retirement. You just take out a Prudential Endowment Assurance.

For example, if you're a man aged 30 next birthday, a monthly premium of £12.50 would give you a guaranteed minimum sum of £5,000 at age 65. But this sum would be increased by bonuses, and a £5,000 policy for a similar term maturing on April 1st, 1974, would have given you a lump sum of £12,970.* Of course, bonuses can go down as well as up. But in the past the trend has always been a steady rise.

For the full story of how to make your retirement secure and happy, just fill in the coupon and send us the card. It won't cost you anything to find out.

And it could give you peace of mind. At the very least.

Prudential

CN/11/73/1240/FP (4529)

Purely by way of interest, I'd like full details of your Endowment Assurance policies.

Name

Address

Prudential Assurance Company Limited

*Applies to U.K. only.

BUSINESS REPLY SERVICE
LICENCE NO.KE 1511

The Chief General Manager
The Prudential Assurance Co Ltd
142 Holborn Bars
London EC1N 2NH

the North-East coast of Scotland, the met forecast was for a bright blue day. As we walked out of the briefing-room I considered that the wind blowing on my face was too cold for the time of the year.

'OK to fly the first sorties?' my Flight Commander asked me.

'No. Keep them on the ground for a bit – until I say fly,' I replied.

The other squadron pilots based on the airfield took off on their first sorties. A quarter of an hour later, fog descended over the airfield with appalling rapidity. It was the dreaded *haar* drifting in from the cold North Sea. They had the greatest difficulty in getting their aircraft down before they ran out of kerosene, and these were then splattered on diversion bases in an area of a hundred miles. That is what instinct is all about.

Fog is, of course, the airman's worst enemy and fog normally occurs in conditions of high air pressure combined with slack winds. The *haar* which encroaches stealthily but with deadly speed over the north eastern coasts of Britain is an unusual phenomenon. Industrial smog brings difficult conditions in terms of slant visibility when, although it is marvellously clear in the skies, forward vision for the purposes of approach and landing might be down to half a mile. But whereas flight either by birds, pterodactyl, or men in their flying machines, is – or was – based on the lift which the Goddess *Aer* provides, she also carries within her bosom the clouds. Cloud formations are the major factor in visually forecasting future weather conditions and these can be categorized, which Theophrastus of Erusus who lived circa 373 BC noted, using such expressions as 'streaks of clouds' and 'clouds like fleeces of wool'. The original met forecaster was Jean Baptiste, a brilliant French biologist, who in 1801–4 systematically classified cloud formations. He invented the titles of the three basic clouds; cirrus, cumulus and stratus; and then went on to propose four additional compound formations; cirro-cumulus, cirro-stratus, cumulo-stratus and cumulo-cirro-stratus or nimbus. These form part of the basis of weather observation today. A sufficient knowledge of the clouds is as important to an aviator as the plumb-line of a seaman sailing in uncharted waters.

Two of the greatest joys I experienced in flight were caused by clouds. On the one hand, a towering cu-nimb, craggy and mountainous, represented a challenge to a pilot in an aerobatic single-seater aircraft watching it from afar. One would open the throttle wide and aim at it, then make a four gee turn to encircle it. It was often worthwhile to plunge into such clouds just for the hell of it. The silence of the cloud after the murmurings of the sky, the consequent invisibility on one's forward progress after the previous absolute clarity of vision was a revelation. The turbulence would suddenly strike, the instrument panel would judder giving one the joyful sensation that one was about to die. Attempting to commit suicide was a pleasurable experience as one dived so fast at these mountains. It was exactly like colliding deliberately with Mount Everest, except that the cu-nimb was comparatively fragile.

But the greatest joy was to cope with the clouds at the finest and most dangerous level – to land through their veiled threats when at the lowest possible altitude – and then touch down on terra firma as a positive act of defiance. Such arts took me twenty years to learn to my satisfaction, but in the end I could land an aircraft such as a Canberra in visibility of a quarter of a mile and with the cloud base at one hundred feet. The sheer difficulty of arriving at this stage of finesse was to fix one's mind to the implicit belief that one's instruments were correctly registering the altitude and air speed of the aircraft throughout the long period when one had no sight of the earth. On the other hand, it was essential not to rely on any single instrument in the cockpit in case it had become unserviceable all unknown to oneself. Accordingly, the information given by the one had to be confirmed by other instruments. This created the need to develop an ability to scan throughout the spectrum of the instrument panel at the speed of light, while still retaining control over the aircraft, and with no outside orientation whatsoever.

When I had conquered these arts, flying for me developed into a new art. The butterflies in the stomach lay quiescent as one opened the throttles when there was a cloud base of a hundred feet and in conditions of visibility of only a quarter of a mile. One would soar through the massed clouds, which were often in layers separated by a few thousand feet, keep the aircraft at a steady angle of climb in the certain knowledge – the almost certain knowledge – that she would eventually crest to one's desired pinnacle. Then like the lotus of Osiris opening to the sun, King *Sol* would blind one with his beaming eye. It was always a traumatic moment; having left the filthy black and gradually exposing grey behind, one was in the brilliance of an azure sky with the sun burning one's face with its heat. People tend to chase the sun – Majorca in July, Madeira in March, Florida at almost any time of the year. I never had to chase the sun; it was always available in the hours of daylight. The whole of Britain might be sulking in conditions of fog or neo fog; I could remain based in Britain and seek solace from the sun at almost any time I so desired – even in December.

The Goddess *Aer* is all-enveloping, all-demanding, and whereas I had managed to keep her at bay for twenty-six years, the effort required to teach all the pilots within my aegis about her magnetism, her charm and deadliness, turned into an insuperable struggle in which I could never have continued to be the victor. When my time came to leave my post as airport manager at the large RAF airfield in Germany, therefore, I came to a clean decision: she and I must part company forever. In any case, I would never have been given another full-time flying appointment in the RAF, so I was merely discounting the inevitable before it occurred. I bided my time, worked out my finances and shot in an application to be retired prematurely from the Air Force. Then I idled my time away, lying in a garden chair, trying not to look up into the blue of the sky, feeling the warmth of the sun on my brow, listening to the hornets purring menacingly above, watching the wasps making dive bombing attacks, while the mosquitoes escorted them in fighter sweeps over my body. *Aer* bore them all in her arms but I had my backside safely planted on a garden chair. I was O.K. I was tranquil as a randy nun looking after a monastery full of young novice monks. I was as quiet as a small baby whose bottom had been rubbed down with talcum powder and covered with a clean nappy but who, all the time, had a boil developing up his anus. There was no doubt about it: the front part of my brain was cleansed of any desire to have further intercourse with my goddess. I had copulated with her for more than six times a day on occasions and she had squeezed me clean and dry as a bone which has been gnawed by a bull-terrier. But where I came unstuck was when Freud took hold of me. The greater part of the brain forms what he described as the unconscious mind, and the front bit, which controls the impulses, is inferior. Then there was another chap by name Franz Anton Mesmer and I should have kept away from him too. He was an Austrian born at Weil in 1733, and he came to the conclusion that the planets possessed a magnetism which affected people, that these were occult forces which controlled the nervous impulses of man.

The air gave me only a few months respite and then came into the attack using its magnetism in the most insidious manner possible. Its charms began to penetrate the unconscious area of my brain which the front part did not necessarily know anything about. The latter was busily controlling my impulses, helping me to beat the mosquitoes to death with monotonous regularity, and this allowed my muses plenty of scope. In consequence, I kept seeing visions and hearing phrases – such as loud-sounding, wine-dark seas; Africa and all her prodigies. *Aer* is a woman all right; a feckless, lascivious whore in fact. She drains one's senses with her loveliness, she is distant yet lecherous; she can be warm and comforting, but at forty-five thousand ft. her temperature descends to minus one hundred degrees. She prefers to get men alone before exercising her hypnotic charm, but if you are stupid enough to lay your head on her milk-filled bosoms, she turns into a shrill shrew. She will allow one to outsoar the shadow of the night and then turn on the full inventory of his bitchiness – hate, calumny, envy and pain. Earth's shadows she will allow to float freely within her aegis, but she will certainly not allow Heaven's light to survive for ever. She is on the one hand a bloodsucking vampire bat; on the other she is full of sweet music and will allow such sounds to creep into the ears; then she cuts the wire and immediately stops the melody.

I was this monk, I thought, this eremite, and she was my hand-maiden – but was she hell! She was Cleopatra lying on her bed succulent and inviting; but she had an asp under the eiderdown. *Son coeur avait ses raisons que la raison ne connait point.* She had seduced two thousand of my colleagues on her four poster bed; and she stuck a dagger in the back of everyone of them. After which she smiled gently, pretending she was not overfond of the salty taste of blood. She is not fair and floral, she is not even fey. She is exactly like another old whore, by name Eskimo Nell – 'And with a sigh, she sucked him dry, With the ease of a vacuum cleaner.'

There were more objects in the air than hornets as I lay back on my garden chair. Apart from the fighter sweeps made by the mosquitoes and the wasps with their dive bombing attacks, there was the groan of jet engines as aircraft thundered away from London Airport, or whispered their way into the circuit in landing configurations. Worse, there were the thick contrails making their appearance and vanishing into thin air at forty thousand feet. Those contrails led to places with strange sounding names – Zanzibar, Tegucigalpa, San José, Port of Spain. I wanted out; yet I wanted in again. The sight of the big jets, VC 10s, Boeing 707s, Comets and DC 8s made my nerve ends come alive. *Aer* then played her final trump card and entered my dreams in the most soothing manner possible, using sirens to entice me back to her bosom, and they number my oracles.

'What about Mandalay,' she suggested, 'where the flying fishes play?' 'Why not accompany me east of Suez where the best is like the worst?' 'Use one of my flying galleons,' she murmured, 'like a whispering VC 10.' 'Surely,' she pointed out, 'you haven't done with me yet? It is obvious to me that you need a further 3,000 opportunities to clamber into my arms? I swear,' she pronounced, 'that I will let you down very gently.' She laid on all the charm of all the muses and I trusted her as far as I could spit. But she is a very persistent whore, very persistent indeed; and when she is not in a state of sulks she is a beautiful woman, nice to live with.

As a part-worn pilot, the only method by which I could get a taste of the air again would be by becoming a (professional) passenger on the international airlines. I was sanguine enough to appreciate that tourist class seats would be highly unsatisfactory, but that first class accommodation would be just bearable, as it was my intention to fly a million miles and visit as many countries in the world as possible. I could not, of course, afford to pay for such facilities but there was a possibility that someone else might pay. It was a long-shot but it came off. I applied to the Foreign Office for an appointment as Queen's Messenger and by the greatest good fortune was selected from a list of candidates as long as my arm. There were about fifty Queen's Messengers when I joined the Corps and their duty was to maintain surveillance of the State secrets contained in diplomatic bags as they were conveyed to every British embassy and High Commission extant. There are approximately 130 such diplomatic posts ranging from Outer Mongolia to Chile and I visited every one, travelling in every major airline in the world. If this was my swan-song, I decided to do it properly.

Some nice judgements were required as, for example, what sort of clothes to pack into the suitcase. In Hong Kong one would simply wear a lightweight suit; from the Crown Colony, however, one would then proceed on to Ulan Bator, capital of Outer Mongolia, where the night temperatures in winter fell to minus 60 degrees. Similar problems had to be faced when travelling on the Central and Latin American routes. Despite the fact that Mexico City lies at about eight thousand feet above sea-level, it is normally hot; but flying from there in a southerly direction for four thousand miles brings one to Santiago, capital of Chile. Chilean winters would make the worst British winters appear to be quite temperate. Then, although Nyeri in Kenya lies directly on the equator, it is on a plateau some five thousand feet high; consequently the nights are cool, cold even, which demanded a thick sweater. On cold nights in cities which are sited at high altitudes, the phenomenon of static electricity has to be experienced to be believed. Put the hand out for the handle of the car door, and a spark three inches long reaches out to grab you and emits a crackle reminiscent of a tiny flash of lightning. In Peking on one dark night I nearly had my hand blown off by the longest flash of static I ever experienced, lightning apart.

I flew my million miles as a passenger, sitting in first-class seats, quite often drinking Charles Heidsieck champagne – my favourite – for free. I admired the air hostesses whose nationalities ranged throughout the whole spectrum of the population of the world; they were all possessed essentially of middle-class values. The international airlines make allowance for about ten per cent of them becoming pregnant each year. I had visions of making the whole hundred per cent pregnant in one year, but I failed dismally in my ambition. Despite their humble mien, the Japanese hostesses, all dressed like the Geishas, bowing and scraping, could have broken my neck with a single karate chop. The best of the lot were Siamese. There is no mystery about sex to the ladies of Thailand; there is just sex.

An American pilot flew me to Kabul, capital of Afghanistan, over the Hindu Kush, having taken off from Teheran in Persia. We flew over the worst terrain in the world, which includes the Persian Salt Desert and the foothills of the Himalayas. Kabul airport did not, at the time, have adequate landing aids according to international standards, and the clouds were filled with snow as we cruised over the Hindu Kush towards Kabul. My goddess came to the conclusion that this might be an appropriate moment to do me in once and for all time, but she was defeated by the American who, fortunately, had at one time been a fighter pilot – only one of such pedigree could have pulled the landing off. He had to make a three gee turn on the final approach and the passengers in the back of the Boeing 727 blacked out. He stuffed the Boeing into reverse thrust when he was at about ten feet up and she hit the ground like a falling brick shithouse. The runway threshold came up so fast that I ducked in anticipation. But he managed to stop her before we ran over the precipice and I took due note that he waited a long time to allow his brakes to cool off before taxiing in. If any one had thrown a bucketful of water over his brakes, the aircraft would have gone up in smoke after the consequent explosion.

She had another go at me when I sat myself in an antiquated Dakota at Lagos and noted with alarm that the pilot was a Negro; not that I have anything against Negroes, merely that I had never before handed my life over to one for safe-keeping. His duty was to keep me breathing until we landed at Dakar, capital of Senegal, overflying territories with romantic sounding names but which are better expressed in the general term 'The White Man's Grave'. This region contains the Slave Coast, the Gold Coast, the Ivory Coast and the Grain Coast. It also contains cumulo-nimbus clouds towering up to 60,000 ft. filled with turbulence of sufficient power as to break up an aircraft in mid-air. The thundery rain that descends in consequence is heavy enough to make holes in the fuselage of an aircraft when on the ground. The Negro would have been hard put to ride a bicycle with aplomb let alone pole a Dakota in these conditions. We landed at Abidjan, Monrovia, Freetown, Conakry, Bathurst and finally at Dakar.

Where my goddess prefers to lose her temper, however, is in the area of the South China Sea. She sometimes hates me as much as I sometimes hate her, so she decided on a once and for all operation when I took off from Manila, capital of the Philippines, in a DC 8 by courtesy of Panam – 'The most experienced airline in the world' – and she brewed up a typhoon in my locality. When I arrived by car at Manila airport the typhoon was merely a hundred miles away and was proceeding steadily at forty knots in my direction. The clouds were grey with their base at about six hundred feet, the wind was beginning to stir the foliage on the trees and I was biting my nails. The skipper hauled the DC 8 off the ground, immediately reduced revs for the climb, and the aircraft staggered up through the cu-nimb like the Great Auk. The turbulence was so ferocious that it seemed in consequence that either my seat-belts would snap, thereby causing my head to burst through the fuselage, or they would retain their hold and cut me in half at about the point of my navel. The crockery in the galley ahead was falling to the floor with monotonous regularity and the senior steward staggered off to the lavatory to be sick in privacy. The Panam air hostesses sat facing me on the horseshoe sofa in the bar, tightly strapped in, teeth gleaming like toothpaste advertisements, because that was what they had been brainwashed into doing come hell or high water.

We were at about fifteen thousand feet, with no prospect of getting out of this cu-nimb until we arrived at forty-five thousand feet, when *Aer* demanded of *Thor* that he must assist her in knocking me off. He obliged with the loudest bang I ever heard in my life, which he followed instantaneously with a bloody great lightning strike; this hit the port inboard engine which was a couple of feet from my head. If I had been looking out of the port window instead of being huddled up in a small ball biting my nails, Thor would, without question, have blinded me.

I thought the time had definitely arrived when I should part company with the air after I had flown on the following route: London Airport to Lisbon, Bermuda, Barbados, Port of Spain, Caracas, Maracaibo, Panama, San Jose, Nicaragua, Tegucigalpa, San Salvador, Merdia to Mexico City and back to Panama again.

Then we proceeded to Bogata, Quito, Lima, La Paz – the highest city in the world – to Santiago. KLM, Royal Dutch Airlines, then assumed responsibility for my body, if not for my soul, and the pilot poled me to Buenos Aires, Montevideo, Rio de Janeiro, across four thousand miles of the South Atlantic until we staged at Lisbon. We then got to Zurich and left for Amsterdam where I changed to a feeder line. I arrived at London Airport precisely five minutes ahead of schedule. The Dutch were always great navigators.

I arrived at my home, woke up screaming in the night, slept again, woke again, and decided that further sleep was impossible. I dressed, went into the garden and dug the good earth. After half an hour's digging, I looked at my watch. The time was 5 o'clock in the moning. My time clock had collapsed and that old bitch *Aer* was directly responsible for this.

So I took the immutable decision to keep away from her. She had by now taken me into her bosom and allowed me to return to earth on more than fifteen thousand occasions. We had been married for nearly thirty years, which was by no means bad considering our incompatibility at the very beginning of it all. Accordingly, I put in my resignation from the job and almost to a man the Foreign Office rejoiced at this. Then I returned to my garden chair and the hornets, wasps and mosquitoes.

I had flown across seven seas and been deposited here and there on the five continents. I now knew almost every trick in the airmanship book. I was so full of knowledge that my brain could assimilate no more. My goddess had borne me, using every airline company whose aircraft flew the international air routes, ranging from Cathay Pacific, through Braniff, Lufthansa, Scandinavian Air Services, Iberian Airways, BOAC, BEA, Air France, TWA, Japanese Air Lines, Chinese Airways, South African Airways, El Al, Panam, Quantas, Air India, Ethiopian Airways and all the rest. In addition, I flew on a hundred feeder-lines.

Like Eskimo Nell, *Aer* had by now sucked me dry.

EPILOGUE

WHEN Shakespeare wrote the prologue to his play *King Henry V*, he used these words: 'The air, a charter'd libertine, is still.' He was very nearly right, but not quite. 'Libertine' at one time was understood as a name given to certain antinomian sects; later the word meant someone who was manumitted from slavery; the truth then drew nearer when it was suggested that libertine described one who is not restrained by moral law, who leads an immoral life, loose in morals, licentious, dissolute, puft, reckless, treading the primrose path of dalliance. These are good words to illustrate *Ae*r, but they are inadequate.

She may be libertine but she is certainly not 'still'; she wants my soul and one day she will get it; then she will meld it with the other billions of souls she already holds. I have a premonition she will make a final, premature and successful effort to grab my soul. She is not just a charter'd libertine; she is all-demanding; she is all-powerful.

Finally, she is a lecherous, seductive, all-embracing old whore. And I love her dearly although I want to have nothing more to do with her.

Aerem expelles furca, tamen usque recurret.

INDEX

Squadron Commander: *see* Allen 'Dizzy', Fisher, James; Gillies, Jasper; and Malan, 'Sailor'
Staff College, 172–3
Staff Officer: Eleven Group HQ, 155–70; Fighter Command HQ, 153, 154
Stanmore, 154–5
Stardust, 26, 47
superstition, 45, 60
Swift aircraft, 172, 181–6

Tangmere, 128–33, 139–41
test flights, 176–86
test pilots, 172, 176–7
Thunderbolt aircraft, 121–3
Tiger moth, 9, 11
Todd, Peter, 36–7
Towers, Group Capt. Tommy, SASO, 155, 159, 162, 165–9
turbulence, 190, 197–8

Twelve Group, 'Dizzy' Gunnery/Tactics Staff Officer at HQ, 124; *see also* East Anglia
Typhoon aircraft, 120

Victory fly past, 130–3

WAAFS, 88–9, 108, 125, 132
weather: Battle of Britain, 56, 58, 75; Coronation Day fly past, 167; Victory fly past, 131; importance in flying, 104, 188–91; *see also* clouds, fog, *haar* and turbulence
West Malling, 75
Williams, batman, 58, 88
Wimsey, Paul, 110–11, 113
Wing Commander, 'Dizzy' promoted to, 155

Yorkshire, East Riding, 126–8